SOCIOLOGY IN FOCUS SERIES
General Editor: Murray Morison

Social Policy

Steve Outram

Senior Lecturer in Sociology,
Staffordshire Polytechnic

LONGMAN
London and New York

LONGMAN GROUP UK LIMITED
Longman House, Burnt Mill, Harlow, Essex CM20 2JE, UK and Associated
Companies throughout the World.

**Published in the United States of America
by Longman Inc., New York.**

© **Longman Group UK Limited 1989**

First published 1989
ISBN 0 582 35533 8

Set in 10/11pt Bembo, Linotron 202

Produced by Longman Group (Far East) Limited
Printed in Singapore

British Library Cataloguing in Publication Data
Outram, Steve
  Social policy. – (Sociology in focus series)
  1. Social policies
  I. Title   II. Series
  361.6'1

  ISBN 0-582-35533-8

Library of Congress Cataloging-in-Publication Data
Outram, Steve.
  Social policy/Steve Outram.
      p.   cm. – (Sociology in focus series)
  Bibliography: p.
  Includes index.
  ISBN 0-582-35533-8
  1. Social policy.   I. Title.   II. Series.
HN18.087   1989   89-2560
361.6'1 – dc20   CIP

Contents

Acknowledgements

I am indebted to Murray for his infinite patience and constructive criticism. I would also like to thank Ursula, Tom and Nim for their love and support.

The publishers are grateful to the following for permission to reproduce copyright material:

Child Poverty Action Group for an extract from the article 'Rural Rides' by Brian McLaughlin in *Poverty* No 63, Spring 1986 and Listener Publications Ltd for an extract from the article 'A Licence to profit from abuse of the elderly' by Mark Halliley in *The Listener* 8.10.87.

Series introduction

Sociology in Focus aims to provide an up-to-date, coherent coverage of the main topics that arise on an introductory course in sociology. While the intention is to do justice to the intricacy and complexity of current issues in sociology, the style of writing has deliberately been kept simple. This is to ensure that the student coming to these ideas for the first time need not become lost in what can appear initially as jargon.

Each book in the series is designed to show something of the purpose of sociology and the craft of the sociologist. Throughout the different topic areas the interplay of theory, methodology and social policy have been highlighted, so that rather than sociology appearing as an unwieldy collection of facts, the student will be able to grasp something of the process whereby sociological understanding is developed. The format of the books is broadly the same throughout. Part 1 provides an overview of the topic as a whole. In Part 2 the relevant research is set in the context of the theoretical, methodological and policy issues. The student is encouraged to make his or her own assessment of the various arguments, drawing on the statistical and reference material provided both here and at the end of the book. The final part of the book contains both statistical material and a number of 'Readings'. Questions have been provided in this section to direct students to analyse the materials presented in terms of both theoretical assumptions and methodological approaches. It is intended that this format should enable students to exercise their own sociological imaginations rather than to see sociology as a collection of universally accepted facts, which just have to be learned.

While each book in the series is complete within itself, the similarity of format ensures that the series as a whole provides an integrated and balanced introduction to sociology. It is intended that the text can be used both for individual and classroom study while the inclusion of the varied statistical and documentary materials lend themselves to both the preparation of essays and brief seminars.

For my Mum and Dad

PART 1

Introduction and overview

1 Introduction

Since the late 1970s the British welfare state has been described as being in a 'state of crisis'. Newspaper stories and television documentaries have continually reported services being reduced, and in some cases lost altogether. Schools have been closed, hospital wards have been 'put in moth balls' because hospital authorities cannot afford to staff them and fewer council houses have been built. All aspects of service have been affected, and the belief that the British welfare state is 'the best in the world' and one which provides support 'from cradle to grave' is now difficult to sustain. For those people who believe that the state has a responsibility for the lives of each citizen, social policy since the late 1970s has come to take on the appearance of a modern-day horror story with government ministers behaving in a monstrous and inhuman way, particularly at a time when the number of unemployed people has reached an unprecedented level and the extent of human need is seen to be at its greatest so far this century (see Figure 1.1).

Alternatively, there are many people who support this re-duction in state welfare provision. They agree with the arguments that welfare provision has become wasteful and, in a period of economic recession, cannot be afforded. They may also agree with the notion that the welfare state has become too large and bureaucratic and has had too much control over their lives. For these people, the alternative of providing for oneself through private schemes such as private health care or private schooling is more desirable because it offers the individual much more 'freedom of choice' in how one provides for oneself and one's dependants. This, they believe, also encourages more competition

Figure 1.1 **Newspaper reports of the 'crisis' in the welfare state**

'HOMELESS CANNOT AFFORD 90 PC OF B & B HOTELS'

Homeless claimants are being priced out of more than 90 per cent of London's cheapest bed and breakfast hotels after the failure of a government free market experiment, according to a survey of over 1000 places to be released today.

The figures – combined with reports from Warwickshire, Buckinghamshire and the South East – show that the Government's maximum £48.30 a week limit is totally inadequate for the majority of claimants.

(*The Guardian*, 25 March 1986)

'SINGLE MOTHER SUFFERS WEEKLY LOSS OF £45'

Judy Richards, a single parent with three children and one of the losers under the new social security system, is striving to adjust to a drop in her weekly income from £71.65 to £26.

The removal of £45 by the Department of Health and Social Security has left 35-year-old Ms Richards with three child allowances at £7.25 plus £4.90 single parent allowance – a total of £26.65.

(*The Guardian*, 21 April 1988)

in what schemes are offered which, in turn, encourages greater efficiency and reduces the cost of social provision.

Another group of people which has been critical of the British welfare state is the group which has direct experience of it; namely, the claimants and recipients of welfare provision. Rather than experiencing welfare agencies as being there to give them help and support, the welfare state has been experienced as brutalising and humiliating. Public administrators such as Supplementary Benefit officers and housing visitors are experienced as agents of social control rather than as people who are concerned with individual welfare; that is, the welfare state is experienced as something which constrains people rather than gives them help. The sheer complexity of welfare bureaucracies and the apparent insensitivity of welfare agents, together with the possible stigma of being a claimant, are sufficient to deter many people from attempting to claim welfare support.

Such an array of opinions and attitudes may provide a potential minefield for the social scientist who attempts to investigate social policy and the welfare state. Clearly, the study of social policy entails entering an arena where moral values and issues of social justice accompany social science analysis; indeed, at times, studies of social policy would seem to have more in common with political manifestos than with social scientific analysis! The tradition of social scientists often being involved in the policy-making process may cast further suspicion on the validity of their analyses since they may appear to be more inclined to satisfy the needs of governments than maintain the tenets of their respective disciplines.

Such issues are particularly important for the sociology student, who is likely to encounter confusion and vagueness concerning the relationship between sociology and social policy. Unlike the history student, who has a well-defined area, that of social history; or even the economics student, who can, for example, readily analyse the annual expenditure on social security; the sociology student is presented with an ill-defined and sometimes contradictory field of study. On the one hand, there is a body of work which argues that, until recently, sociologists were not interested in social policy and the few sociologists who did attempt a sociological analysis of social policy were peripheral to the mainstream developments in the subject. Instead, the study of social policy was seen to be the province of 'social administration', which has a much more practical concern than that of the more theoretically concerned sociologist. On the other hand, there are those sociologists who have argued that a concern with social policy has often been implicit in sociological analysis. Such people would point to areas such as education or poverty, where the policy implications of streaming, for example, or of 'the poverty trap', are quite clear.

Since the late 1970s two developments have taken place which have had strong implications for the development of a sociological analysis of social policy. First, in 1979 a Conservative government was elected which held quite a different attitude to social policy and the welfare state from any previous post-war government. No longer was it possible to take for granted continued state support for welfare provision. Second, there were developments in sociological analysis which had clear implications for any subsequent discussion of social policy and the welfare state. One of these was the development by Marxist sociologists of new ideas about the nature of the capitalist state, including the capitalist state's involvement in social welfare. For example, it was demonstrated that the welfare state in capitalist society may serve to support a healthy labour force and also provide ideological legitimation of the state's activities at the same time as providing a measure of social control over the labour force. To that extent it has been argued that the welfare state is a major arena of class struggle.

The second of these developments was the demonstration by feminist analyses that women were 'invisible' in most sociological accounts. **Margaret Stacey**, for example, argued in *The division of labour re-visited or overcoming the two Adams* (in P. Abrams *et al* (eds), *Practice and Progress: British Sociology 1950–1980*, Allen & Unwin, 1981) that sociologists had been primarily concerned with investigating the public world of the state and of the market-place and had largely ignored the private world of the home. This has very important implications for the sociology of social policy since it is the world of the family and the home where social policies have had most influence and it is women in the home who are most likely to be responsible for the social welfare of others.

It is the object of this book, therefore, to introduce some of the sociological issues that are raised in attempting to understand and analyse social policy and the welfare state – traditional issues such as the relationship between sociology and social policy; issues which are central to sociology such as value freedom, and socio-logical issues which have a particular application to the study of social policy such as class conflict and social control. Finally, developments since the late 1970s have led to the introduction of new issues and a need to reconsider such areas as social inequality and the state, and some authors have suggested that there is now a 'new social policy'.

2 The study of social policy

Since social policy is a *field of study* rather than a discrete socio-logical topic such as deviance or social class, the contributions of economists and political scientists have a bearing on discussions of social policy. Economic considerations are central to any analysis of social policy because most social policies are concerned with the distribution of resources in society. Social policy is generated in the political system, and it is important to examine the political and moral values of the groups of people engaged in all areas of this process: the legislators and the administrators such as housing managers and social security officers; and the people who are affected by social policies – which includes most of us since we are all affected by social policies at some time in our lives.

Why study social policy?

There are several important reasons for studying social policy.

1 As **Michael Hill** suggests in *Understanding Social Policy* (Basil Blackwell, 2nd edn, 1983) the study of social policy is important for those people who may be involved in the policy process such as social workers, health visitors, housing managers and so on. They may use studies of social policy to inform their practices and improve the delivery of services. In this sense, the study of social policy entails a pragmatic concern with the satisfaction of people's needs.

2 Since the development of what we know as the British welfare state after 1945, social policies have had a strong influence on the British social structure. The life chances of all of us are affected by changes in policies; by giving or removing support and by regulating many aspects of our lives.

3 The analysis of social policy, as with sociology in general,

entails an examination of moral values. By studying social policy one may reflect on one's own values and beliefs as well as considering the values of those people who have the power to influence the creation and implementation of policies. In addition to the values of politicians we may also consider the *discretionary power* of those people responsible for the delivery of services and who decide who will receive a service and what sort of service they will receive. By studying social policy, therefore, the sociologist can render a view of the world which contributes to the more general discussion of the role of values in society and in sociological analysis; indeed, **Robert Pinker** suggests that

> in the discipline of social policy and administration most of the central value-problems of general sociology are dramatically heightened and amplified.
> (R. Pinker, *Social Theory and Social Policy*, Heinemann Educational Books, 1971)

4 Since the 1970s social policy and the operation of the welfare state have been increasingly criticised as being wasteful and unfair. Many of the basic tenets that form the moral justification for social welfare have been challenged, such as freedom from want or the necessity of state provision in housing, health and education. By applying the sociological skills of theory and research we may examine the nature and operation of social policies and make valid and verifiable observations which enable us to evaluate the various claims made for and against the existence of a welfare state.

The study of social policy, therefore, enables us to improve our understanding of our own lives as well as the lives of other people in the community. Further, by making these observations, the sociologist may have a direct or indirect influence on future policies. As **Richard Titmuss** reminded us, social policy implies action, and as **C. Wright Mills** argued, to make sociological statements is to adopt a moral and political position:

> It is the political task of the social scientist . . . continually to translate personal troubles into public issues, and public issues into the terms of their human meaning for a variety of individuals.
> (C. Wright Mills, *The Sociological Imagination*, Pelican Books, 1970)

There is a danger, however, that the study of social policy becomes no more than a political discussion which reveals more about our own values than it does about the nature of social policy in society. In an analysis of housing policy, for example, we may be more concerned to express our own opinions on whether it is right or wrong to 'sell off' council houses than with examining why that policy was introduced and what effects it has had on housing markets and people's lives. Obviously, we cannot suspend our own beliefs and values – no student can do that, whether he or she is a sociology student or a law student or even a physics student. We can, however, adopt a number of practices with which to guard against our studies being no more than an expression of political ideas.

First, we can analyse the success or failure of a policy *in its own terms*. The Conservative government White Paper on Housing which was published in 1973, for example, states quite clearly that

> The ultimate aim of housing policy is that everyone should have a decent home with a reasonable choice of renting or owning the sort of house they want.
>
> (HMSO, *Widening the Choice – the Next Step in Housing*, Cmnd. 5280, 1973)

Not only has the number of homeless families increased during the 1980s but the English Housing Condition Survey showed in 1981 that over 1 million of the 18.1 million dwellings in England were considered unfit for human habitation. Clearly, the aim of housing policy as stated in 1973 has yet to be realised (see Figure 2.1).

Second, we may develop an analysis of social policy that goes beyond our own experiences and beliefs by qualifying our statements with *evidence*. This may be derived from a number of sources: we can undertake our own research; we can use *statistical data* taken from national surveys such as the General Household Survey; we can adopt a *case study* method, perhaps entailing some form of *action research*; and so on. The importance of research evidence in the sociology of social policy cannot be overstated, otherwise we leave ourselves open to the criticism that we are using sociology to conceal support for a political group or party.

Third, a further guard against uncritical value-judgements is to ensure that our analysis of social policy is theoretically sound; that is, the concepts and ideas of the social sciences should be

Figure 2.1 **Housing**
Nic Madge illustrates the deterioration in housing provision.

Although the effect of the right-to-buy provisions has now taken the number of public sector dwellings to below 6.5 million, the present Government continues its push to see as much as possible of the remaining stock sold off wholesale. The Secretary of State for the Environment has welcomed as 'very sensible' a Private Member's Bill sponsored by John Pawley MP which would compel councils to sell off empty properties.

In the International Year of Shelter for the Homeless the number of people in England applying to local authorities for help with accommodation has reached a new peak of over 250 000, with about 100 000 accepted annually for rehousing.

(Nic Madge, 'Recent developments in housing law', *Legal Action*, June 1987)

employed to present logical arguments in relation to social policy. Consider the following assertions:

Social security is a system which encourages idleness and irresponsibility, and discourages initiative and enterprise.
(Nigel Lawson, Chancellor of the Exchequer, Scottish Conservative Party Conference, 10 May 1985)

The new supplementary benefit scheme introduced by the Tories is harsh and unfair.
(Labour Party Election Manifesto, 1983, p. 19)

The sociologist who attempts to evaluate these competing claims must gather the available evidence on the operation of the social security system. Further, this analysis must state clearly what is meant by 'irresponsibility' and 'unfair' since there are differing notions of what is meant by responsibility and differing notions of what is socially just.

What is social policy?

There is no simple and straightforward definition of social policy; indeed, **Alan Walker** has suggested that there are almost as many definitions of social policy as the number of people writing about it (see Figure 2.2). As **Michael Hill** and **Glen Bramley** point out:

> Many people would begin by listing certain labels given to public policies or services, asserting that a particular group of these constitute social policy. The initial lists would certainly include:
> 1 Social security (income maintenance, pensions, national insurance benefits etc.);
> 2 health services;
> 3 welfare or personal social services;
> Most people would include education, and many would mention housing.
> (Michael Hill and Glen Bramley, *Analysing Social Policy*, Basil Blackwell, 1986)

This type of classification of social policy often focuses on the *institutions* involved in service delivery and often goes no further than a descriptive history of the respective social policies – in 1870 the Forster Education Act introduced a national system of elementary education; the Butler Education Act of 1944 introduced universal secondary education, and so on.

We may be critical of this approach in several ways. First, it lacks any theoretical analysis. For example, we never get to know why these Acts were introduced or who benefited from their introduction. Second, this approach leads to a conflation of social policy with the welfare state; that is, they are treated as if they were the same thing, yet many aspects of social policy are found outside what we know as the welfare state. Richard Titmuss, for example, argued that we need to look at *occupational welfare* – the benefits such as pension schemes, help with housing costs, company cars, support for a child's private education, support with private health plans and so on, that some individuals receive from their employers. A third criticism of this approach is that it divorces discussions of social policy from discussions of economic policy even though, in practice, they are closely related. This, in turn, leads to the view that social policy is secondary to economic policy, that we can only afford to build new houses and hospitals and so on in a period of economic growth. In periods of economic decline or recession this view holds that welfare spending is likely to be cut. Yet, as Alan Walker has argued, it is just as valid to argue that social policies and the satisfaction of needs should take priority over economic concerns (see Figure 2.2). A further criticism of this approach is that it is difficult to undertake *comparative analysis* of social policy. Comparative analysis of social security in Britain and the United States of America, for example, would enable us to extend our sociological understanding of the relationship between social policy and social structure as well as contributing to the debates about which policies are successful and which are unlikely to succeed (see Figure 2.2).

Figure 2.2 **The scope of social policy**
Social policy embraces much more than welfare provision, as the following extracts demonstrate.

> There are social policies in South Africa today which many people would not regard as being beneficient or welfare oriented. There are social insurance programmes in some Latin American countries, Brazil in particular, which function as concealed multipliers of inequality. . . . Hitler developed social policies in Nazi Germany concerning the mentally ill and retarded, the Jews and other ethnic groups.
> (R. Titmuss, *Social Policy*, George Allen & Unwin, 3rd impression, 1974)

Similarly, Evan Stone considered National Service and conscription to be an aspect of social policy:

> . . . owing to the political situation and Great Britain's commitments overseas, successive governments have considered that it was necessary to retain national service in peace time.
> (Evan Stone 'National Service', in P. Archer (ed.), *Social Welfare and the Citizen*, Penguin Books, 1957)

He goes on to describe the responsibilities of employers to re-employ their employees who have undertaken a period of National Service, concluding:

> This is one more instance of the way in which those who are called upon to serve the community are protected as befits its members.
> (Ibid.)

More recently, a number of commentators have called for a 'social policy for work'. That is, jobs should be created not on the basis that they might improve economic growth, but on the basis that jobs are needed to meet the needs of the unemployed.

> Policy-makers serious about reducing unemployment must embark on some form of job creation. Without a positive policy to reduce unemployment all of the other progressive objectives of social policy are called into question, not least by the demands on resources to pay even basic subsistence benefits. In other words, without an employment policy the future of welfare is very bleak indeed.
> (A. Walker 'Sharing the job shortage', in R. Klein and M. O'Higgins (eds). *The Future of the Welfare State*, Basil Blackwell, 1985)

Although there are many definitions of social policy, it is possible to identify a number of common themes, as Alan Walker does in *Social Planning – a Strategy for Socialist Welfare*. Walker suggests that the dominant theme is the

> idea of collective, or state, intervention in the private market to promote individual welfare.
> (Alan Walker, *Social Planning – a Strategy for Socialist Welfare*, Basil Blackwell, 1984)

That is, the state intervenes in the lives of individuals in order to give support. This intervention takes place within the context of a capitalist or market economy. The British economy, therefore, may be described as a mixed economy where private markets and production (such as manufacturing industries) and services (such as banking) exist in which the prime objective is making a profit, and a public sector exists which has the prime objective of satisfying social and individual need. Most accounts of social policy hold the assumption that people have needs, and, in a mixed economy, there are likely to be occasions when state provision is the best, if not the only, means of satisfying those needs. Housing, for example, is very expensive to buy in the private market and, for many people, applying for council accommodation may be the only opportunity they have of living in a decent home.

A second recurrent theme in any definition of social policy, therefore, is that of *need*. Needs occur at both individual and societal levels. For example, the system of social security operates to satisfy an individual or family need for an income. Similarly, part of the job of water authorities is to ensure that the community's water supply is not polluted. However, there is no simple definition of what constitutes a need and some authors have argued that any definition of need is itself a political statement. It is certainly the case that in recent years the identification of needs has been strongly related to pressure-group activities. For example, the needs of older people have been defined and expressed by such organisations as Age Concern and Help the Aged.

The provision of social services and social support has to be paid for, and another theme, one that has become increasingly important, has been the examination of the collection and distribution of welfare resources. The main sources of funding are National Insurance, local community charges and taxes. Once collected, governments have to decide on the allocation of funds, both to different sectors of the state and to different individuals and groups in society. Governments have to decide whether defence is more important than welfare and whether education is more important than housing; they have to decide whether to increase taxes and National Insurance payments in order to spend more on these items or whether to decrease these payments in order to allow greater individual freedom of choice in spending. Similarly, many services, such as housing and education, are administered by local authorities who have similar choices to make. In recent years this has led to a conflict between governments that have wished to reduce spending on social welfare and some local authorities that have preferred to increase spending.

Social policy, then, is concerned with assuming responsibility for people's needs and creating the means by which resources and services are allocated to meet those needs. This implies that social policy is concerned with the amelioration of individual and social problems. As **Vic George** and **Paul Wilding** suggest in *Ideology and Social Welfare*, (Routledge & Kegan Paul, rev. edn, 1985) ideas about social problems and subsequent social policies are inter-related. The study of social policy must include an examination of the ways in which 'social problems' come to be defined as such. A number of studies have demonstrated, for example, that in the Middle Ages many people were poor in Britain, but it was not considered to be a social problem. These studies go on to show that systems of poverty relief were introduced, not so much out of a humanitarian concern for the well-being of the poor, but in order to regulate an increasingly unreliable workforce; that is, poverty relief was introduced to serve the interests of landowners rather than ameliorate individual hardship. In a similar way we must question contemporary social policies and consider whose best interests are being served. Many claimants and welfare re-cipients, for example, experience the welfare state as something which extends state control over their lives without doing much to satisfy their needs; they point to the difficulty of knowing what it is that they may be entitled to; they complain of the treatment that they receive by officials and the shame of being labelled as a 'scrounger'. A common complaint made by social security claimants of the people who administer benefits is that 'they behave as if it were their own money they were giving you' rather than benefits to which an individual is entitled because of the National Insurance contributions they made when they were employed.

Sociology and social policy

Historically, the study of social policy was essentially the preroga-tive of social administration rather than sociology. Robert Pinker suggests that sociology originated as a critical response to the development of capitalist industrialism. The sociological tradition which subsequently developed was essentially theoretical, entailing attempts at explaining social change. The study of social policy, on the other hand, was seen to be an 'applied' social science with a separate moral concern with securing reform; as Pinker states: In social policy and administration we begin with fact finding and end in moral rhetoric' (Robert Pinker, *Social Theory and Social Policy*, Heinemann Educational Books, 1971). He goes on to suggest that the early 'founding fathers' of sociology – Durkheim, Spencer, Marx and Weber – had only an incidental interest in social policy. Social administration, as this applied social science came to be known, and sociology, therefore, have developed in quite different ways. Although much of sociology has an implicit concern with policy – for example, in the sociology of education – it has had a primary aim of *explaining* the nature of social life and social change (see Figure 2.3).

Social administration, however, has had a primary aim of *demonstrating · areas of need and securing policy reforms*. The people

Figure 2.3 **Social policy and the 'early sociologists'**
The view that the 'founders' of sociology had only an implicit interest in social policy is not shared by all commentators. For example, Graham Room argues that both Weber and Durkheim had a clear concern with social policy:

> Weber in particular was concerned to emphasise the positive role of the state: as an agent of life chance distribution, as an instigator of societal change and as a promoter of social integration. He saw social policies as central to this role.

Similarly, Room argues that Durkheim was overtly concerned with social policy.

> [Durkheim] saw the rise of the state – intervening in life-chance distribution, promoting the division of labour and societal advance and pursuing social integration – as the 'normal' concomitant to advancing industrialisation.
> (Graham Room, *The Sociology of Welfare: Social Policy, Stratification and Political Order*, Basil Blackwell & Mott, 1979)

engaged in the study of social policy were also active in the policy-making process. They held an optimistic belief that there .was a consensus concerning the improvement of everyone's life and that with the correct policies a better society could be achieved.

> They were united above all by a shared vision of a more equal, more just society, with 'better' social services financed through redistributive taxation. Scholarship and advocacy co-existed easily in this consensual world.
> (P. Wilding, 'The evolution of social administration', in P. Bean and S. Macpherson (eds), *Approaches to Welfare*, Routledge & Kegan Paul, 1983)

Sociologists have been critical of social administration for being ameliorative and lacking any body of theory; social administration has been critical of sociology for being too abstract and idealistic. For example, **Hilary Rose** describes how, in the 1960s, the sociologists at the London School of Economics 'distanced themselves' from the Department of Social Science and Administration, jokingly referring to the latter as the 'Department of Applied Virtue'; as she says:

> Sociology's enthusiasm to be seen doing 'real sociology' facilitated a neglect and even avoidance of the sociology of social policy. While the sociology of religion, education, work, deviancy, social stratification, etc. were legitimate areas of study, poverty and the welfare state were not.
> (H. Rose, 'Re-reading Titmuss: the sexual division of welfare', *Journal of Social Policy*, part 10, no. 4, 1981)

She further suggests that an important reason for this separation was the 'gendering' of social science; that is, that a concern with welfare and caring for others was seen to be essentially 'women's work' within sociology departments and was accorded less academic status than 'real sociology'.

The social administration tradition

The traditional social administration approach to the study of social policy is one that has a practical concern with finding solutions to social problems. For example, the social scientist may identify a problem such as homelessness and demonstrate a need for better housing provision. Its starting point, therefore, is often the collection of statistical material with which to refute normative or commonsense assumptions about society. For example, it was generally thought that by the 1960s poverty in Britain had been largely eradicated. However, a number of influential pieces of research demonstrated that widespread deprivation continued to exist. The principal methodological approach of social administration is the use of social surveys. Further, its focus is largely piecemeal and parochial. This approach leads to the identification of particular needy groups or individuals and is prescriptive in recommending specific policy reforms, but it does not attempt to connect the whole range of needs and problems in capitalist society within a comprehensive social theory. Consequently, social administration tends to concentrate on government policies and institutions. Further, because it lacks any theoretical foundation of its own it has tended to be academically eclectic, borrowing concepts and ideas from the other social sciences. The outcome is the development of a tradition which is identified more by its practitioners than its theoretical analysis. **P. Taylor-Gooby**, for example, suggests that 'An impressive heritage stretches back through Donnison, Townsend, Titmuss to Beveridge, the Webbs, and Rowntree, Booth and earlier Chadwick, Kay-Shuttleworth and John Simon' (P. Taylor-Gooby, 'The empiricist tradition in social administration', *Critical Social Policy*, 1(2), Autumn 1981).

According to **Vic George** this consensual, pragmatic and reformist approach to social policy changed very little until the 1970s. He suggests five reasons for the development of a critique of social administration at this time. First, social administration started to engage in some self-criticism for its lack of theory, and there was a recognition that the collection of empirical data without any theoretical foundation was to be uncritically empiricist in the analysis of social policy. Second, George suggests that the political consensus of the 1950s and 1960s was replaced in the 1970s by increasing concern about the 'proper role of the state'. Third, he cites the increasing economic crisis in Britain in the late 1970s as a signal for the end of welfare expansion. This had the effect of reducing welfare spending and increasing the amount of discretion entailed in resource allocation, resulting in the political nature of resource allocation being much more apparent and public. A fourth reason was the growing evidence that welfare provision was having little impact on meeting social needs and reducing social inequalities. Finally, George suggests that changes took place in the nature of academic sociology in the 1970s. There was the development of new ideas about the state, leading to an interest by sociologists in the welfare state. The Marxist and feminist analyses of state welfare which developed at this time undermined the traditional assumption of social administration that the welfare state is necessarily a 'good thing'.

The 'new social policy'

The reappraisal by sociologists of state welfare as a valuable object of enquiry has led to a much wider and more critical study of social policy. This broader scope extends to an analysis of the relationship between social policy and social structure, and the ways in which social policy affects all of our lives.

Marxism and social policy

There are several ways in which Marxist sociology has contributed to the development of the study of social policy. In particular, the development of ideas within Marxism has facilitated a new examination of the relationship between *social class and social policy*; similarly, Marxist analyses of *the state in capitalist society* have enabled us to reconsider the nature and role of the welfare state and Marxist ideas about political economy have been used to re-examine the economics of social policy. Within this new approach to the study of social policy we may also examine the extent to which the welfare state may be considered as an *ideological state apparatus* which serves to secure the legitimacy of continued inequalities in capitalist societies.

Feminism and social policy

The development of feminism within sociology in the 1970s has also had an impact on the study of social policy. Not only have feminists been critical of the social administration approach, they have also criticised Marxist analyses for being 'blind' to the importance of women in any analysis of social welfare and social policy. They have argued that the sociology of social policy, as with sociology in general, has ignored the importance of women, yet women are central to any examination of the development of the British welfare state and the nature of contemporary social policy. Women were important in the establishment of social welfare and continue to be important – not only in influencing the formulation of policy but also as welfare workers and as welfare recipients. Women undertake the bulk of welfare work in Britain as paid workers such as teachers, nurses, social workers, and community workers. They also undertake most of the unpaid welfare work as wives and mothers in the family and as voluntary workers in the community.

Recent changes in sociology, therefore, have had a significant influence on the study of social policy leading us to question many of the assumptions that have been taken for granted about the nature of the welfare state and social inequality in contemporary Britain.

PART 2

Social policy and the welfare state

3 Social policy and social inequality

It is a widely held belief that social policies and the welfare state reduce social inequalities by distributing goods and services to those in need, paid for by the relatively 'better-off' and the wealthy. State intervention in education, housing, health and incomes is considered to be *egalitarian*; that is, it promotes equality or, at least, serves to reduce inequality. It would seem to be a straightforward sociological task, therefore to examine whether social policies have had this effect. We may examine housing need and the distribution and allocation of housing stock and see how far housing policies have had an impact on securing a decent home for everyone. However, two issues make this apparently straight-forward task more difficult. First, we must examine what exactly is meant by 'equality'; and second, we must examine the intended and unintended consequences of social policies.

What is equality?

Julian Le Grand suggests 'five distinct types of equality' that can be identified in social policy:

1 *Equality of public expenditure*: public expenditure should be provided to each individual equally. For example, resources allocated to each school pupil should be the same regardless of abilities or needs.

2 *Equality of final income*: public expenditure should be directed at those who have most initial need. For example, the provision of student grants makes it possible for working-class children to

enter higher education alongside their middle-class peers, although there is no guarantee that their achievements will be the same once they have entered higher education.

3 *Equality of use*: expenditure should be directed so that 'relevant individuals' receive roughly the same service. For example, a working-class person suffering from a particular complaint in one part of the country should receive the same service as a middle-class person suffering from the same complaint in another part of the country.

4 *Equality of cost*: as Le Grand points out, this is more often described as *equality of access* or *equal opportunity*, and refers to the allocation of provision where we all have the same opportunity of receiving a service.

> The requirement that all individuals should have equal access to a service can be most easily interpreted as implying that the costs to all individuals of using that service (per unit) should be equal; for if two individuals wishing to use the service face different costs of doing so, then access to that service has been unequal.
> (Julian Le Grand, *The Strategy of Equality – Redistribution and the Social Services*, George Allen & Unwin, 1982)

5 *Equality of outcome*: public provision should be allocated in order that we are all equal after a service has been delivered. For example, education spending should be so allocated that all pupils leave the education system with roughly similar skills. In a limited way the system of *positive discrimination* that was introduced in Educational Priority Areas following the Plowden Report in 1967 illustrates this view: primary schools in disadvantaged areas were able to claim extra resources so that all pupils would be in a similar position on entering secondary schools. (The term 'positive action' is now often preferred to 'positive discrimination' since 'discrimination' suggests a degree of unfairness.)

Further, as **Anthony Forder** states in *Concepts in Social Administration: a Framework for Analysis* (Routledge & Kegan Paul, 1974), the redistribution of goods and services through social welfare may occur in different directions; throughout an individual's life; between individuals; between different time periods; and between different areas. Each of these is a concern of social policy. For example, if it is acknowledged that there is a need for new houses, governments have to decide whether to build a large quantity of poorer quality houses that will not last thirty years or whether to build fewer houses of better quality. Local authorities then have to decide what proportion of houses, if any, will be designed to meet particular needs such as those of older people or the disabled. Having built these houses, they then have to select which particular individuals will be allocated to them.

Political ideologies and social policy

In making these choices politicians are guided by a set of values and beliefs about what is fair. These values are likely to be a part of a more general world-view or philosophy that we all use to justify a particular set of actions. Politicians, even within the same political party, have differing outlooks on what is socially just. Although there are variations, a number of central political ideologies can be identified which have influenced the development of social policy in Britain.

Equality and freedom

A central issue in any political ideology is the relationship between equality and freedom. For some, equality and freedom are antithetical; that is, one is gained at the expense of the other. For example, state regulation of education or housing leads to a higher degree of planning which, in turn, leads to a curtailment of our individual freedom to live in the sort of house we want or to educate our children as we would like. Other people, however, believe that the promotion of freedom can only be achieved by policies which reduce inequalities. Beveridge, for example, maintained that freedom must include freedom from 'want and squalor' and other social evils. That is, state regulation is necessary to promote equality and enhance personal freedom. Thus, a person who does not have sufficient income to lead the sort of life that we consider to be appropriate in our society, such as sending Christmas cards or having a television set, is unable to participate fully in the community.

Two influential studies of social policy and political ideology are *Ideology and Social Welfare* by **Vic George** and **Paul Wilding**

(Routledge & Kegan Paul, rev. edn, 1985), and *The Sociology of Welfare* by G. Room (Basil Blackwell & Mott, 1979) and it is useful to examine some of their ideas.

Political liberalism – the reluctant collectivists

By 'collectivism' is meant the belief that all members in a community have a responsibility to one another, including sharing the costs of meeting other people's needs. In contrast, individualism is used to refer to the belief that everyone should be personally responsible for themselves. According to George and Wilding, reluctant collectivists (who are very similar in description to Room's 'political liberals') are essentially pragmatic.

> Their pragmatism is the product of the conviction that capitalism is not self-regulating. They continue to believe that it is the best economic system, but they believe that to function efficiently and fairly, it requires judicious regulation and control. Its faults are serious, but they can be corrected.
> (V. George and P. Wilding, *Ideology and Social Welfare*, Routledge & Kegan Paul, rev. edn, 1985)

The central policy goal of reluctant collectivists such as Keynes and Beveridge was to secure full employment. They believed that the inequalities inherent in a capitalist society are necessary and desirable to promote competition and preserve individual freedom. However, they also recognised that, if left unchecked, the inequalities that capitalism engenders would become excessive, leading to social division and conflict. The role of social policy and the welfare state, therefore, is to regulate the economy, albeit in a minimal way, in order to facilitate the smooth running of capitalist society. In that sense they may be considered as collectivistic, but reluctantly so.

Among the principal adherents to this set of ideas after the Second World War were Keynes, whose economic ideas were very influential, and Beveridge, whom many consider to be the principal architect of the British welfare state. They viewed unemployment as the biggest 'social evil' because, following the experiences of the economic depression in the 1920s and 1930s, unemployment was considered to be destructive and wasteful.

Reluctant collectivism, therefore, is *reformist*. Supporters of this set of values do not see a role for social policy in producing a more equal society, nor do they wish to see an end to capitalism. Rather, they believe that society is largely harmonious, with a high degree of consensus in values and political beliefs. However, the operation of capitalism, with its booms and slumps, may create pockets of extreme hardship which threaten this consensus and order. Piecemeal reforms are necessary to restore harmony without fundamentally changing the social and economic system. As the Beveridge reforms in the 1940s illustrate, social security was extended not to equalise incomes and wealth in society but to support poor people *at subsistence levels* until such time as they were able to find a job. 'They' in this instance refers generally to men, since it was assumed by Beveridge that women would get married and stay at home, being dependent on their husbands for their 'living'.

Reluctant collectivism may be located in the context of a wider political liberalism, which holds that individual freedom is central to democracy and that in industrial societies there is a gradual evolution or improvement. There is little, if any, consideration of class conflict in this view, let alone structural inequalities based on gender, race and generation. Rather, there is the belief that any conflict will decline as societies evolve; and it is the important job of government to implement whatever policies are necessary to protect this evolution and social integration. That is, social policies are intended to reduce social conflict by providing support for people who otherwise might question the existing social order (see Figure 3.1).

Social democracy – the Fabian socialists

George and Wilding argue that socialism is difficult to define because it is surrounded by a variety of political and theoretical perspectives. However, Fabianism is defined by two central propositions: 'total commitment to the democratic process and the unequivocal support for social welfare' (ibid.). George and Wilding suggest that equality, freedom and co-operation are fundamental Fabian beliefs. These beliefs, in turn, lead to a concern with democracy, efficiency, the personal development of the individual and with 'natural justice'. For the Fabians, equality is a necessary precondition of freedom: unless everyone enjoys a measure of equality they are 'in bondage' to someone else and therefore unable to control their own lives. An important aspect

Figure 3.1 **Social policy and social integration**
In discussing the views of social policy held by political
liberals, Graham Room relates how they see social policy
having an important role in facilitating social integration.

. . . social policies are among the most significant factors
making for this civic reintegration of the labour force.
They help to promote an identity of interest among all
social groups and have rendered irrational as well as
anachronistic any life project that looks to collective
revolutionary action on the part of the working class for
the achievement of its goals. Instead, the atomised indi-
vidualistic pursuit of occupational 'status' and of income
has become the norm.
(Graham Room, *The Sociology of Welfare: Social Policy,
Stratification and Political Order*, Basil Blackwell & Mott;
Martin Robertson, 1979)

of Fabian thought, therefore, is the promotion of social rights and
a sense of duty. For **T. H. Marshall**, social rights are central to
the development of *citizenship* in a democratic society. That is,
having achieved political and legal rights, individuals should be
granted rights to social welfare. Just as we have the fundamental
right to vote in an election, or the fundamental right to a fair trial,
so Marshall contended we should have the fundamental right to
enjoy a reasonable standard of living. Social rights differ from
civil rights, as **Graham Room** explains. Social rights are

publicly defined and guaranteed claims to certain life chance
outcomes; notably those distributed through the contemporary
social services.
(Graham Room, *The Sociology of Welfare: Social Policy, Stratification and Political Order*, Basil Blackwell & Mott; Martin
Robertson, 1979)

Social policy and the welfare state, therefore, are crucial to the
Fabian pursuit of the gradual and peaceful transition to a socialist
society. For Fabians, redistribution through the welfare state, as
a matter of right rather than patronage or discretion, not only

Figure 3.2 **Fabianism and justice**

V. George and P. Wilding describe the Fabians' attitude to 'natural justice':

> Gross inequalities offend against ideas of natural justice because they lead to a denial of natural rights when, for example, educational opportunities are distributed not according to ability but according to the accidents of birth and parental income. They also violate ideas of natural justice because they endow a minority lavishly, not as a result of its contribution to the common good but because of birth and inheritance. Clearly, the basis of this objection is the assumption that all human beings have certain natural rights which should be respected by society.
>
> (V. George and P. Wilding, *Ideology and Social Welfare* Routledge & Kegan Paul, rev. edn, 1985)

serves to reduce inequalities, thereby securing a greater measure of social justice, but it also fosters a sense of altruism and community within society (see Figure 3.2). For example, **Richard Titmuss** in *The Gift Relationship* (Allen & Unwin, 1970) examined the blood donor system in Britain where individuals freely and anonymously give help to strangers. He concluded that social policy and social improvement were underpinned by a sense of duty, the principle of altruism and the gift relationship. This case illustrates the humanitarian aspect of Fabianism: that everyone should enjoy a reasonable standard of living, and that individual needs should be met wherever possible. Like the reluctant collectivists, they see social policy as a means for opposing the inequalities in capitalist society. However, their social policy goals extend much further in that they see social policy as a means for gradually transforming society into one where a socialist ethic of equality and co-operation prevails rather than the individualism and competitive inequality of capitalism. (The use of social policy to change society is sometimes known as *social engineering*.)

Market liberalism, monetarism and the 'New Right'

Market liberalism, or 'anti-collectivism', as George and Wilding refer to it, differs from the previous two ideologies in the propositions that most welfare spending is (1) wasteful, (2) unfair and (3) a limitation on our personal freedom of choice. Market liberals believe that governments should not interfere with the running of the economy; rather, market forces – that is, the fluctuations that result from supply and demand – should be allowed to determine which enterprises succeed and which fail. This philosophy was dominant in Britain in the nineteenth century, and when referring to this period commentators speak of *laissez-faire* or 'let things be' – meaning, 'let things alone, don't interfere'. It was largely superseded in the twentieth century with the development and continued commitment to the welfare state by political liberals and social democrats or Fabians. However, when in 1979 Margaret Thatcher's Conservative government was elected, with quite a different attitude towards welfare spending, commentators detected a shift in the political consensus and a widespread belief that these ideas had failed. The new Conservative administration believed that the economic ideas of *monetarism* were more valid than the Keynesian model of regulating the economy to achieve a balance between inflation and unemployment.

In the late 1970s, with rising inflation and unemployment, many voters were persuaded that it was time for a complete change in government thinking. Monetarists such as Milton Friedman and Frederick Hayek argued that the levy of taxes to support welfare spending acts as a disincentive to entrepreneurs and innovators, who provide the impetus for expansion and the creation of new jobs. They held that much of welfare spending is wasted money since it services large, monopolistic organisations such as the National Health Service and supports people who could look after themselves. They go so far as to argue that the level of social support may be so high that it encourages many people to remain unemployed. Further, state welfare restricts our freedom – for example, in our choice of health care or schooling (see Figure 3.3).

The Conservative governments under Margaret Thatcher were strongly influenced by these ideas, which are sometimes referred to as 'Thatcherism' or 'the New Right'. Modern market liberals are not opposed to the idea of a welfare state as such, but they

Figure 3.3 **Welfare and the New Right**
The 'New Right' attitude to welfare is succinctly summarised by Milton and Rose Friedman, talking of welfare in America, although it applies just as well to Britain. They say:

> Most of the present welfare programs should never have been enacted. If they had not been, many people now dependent on them would have become self-reliant individuals instead of wards of the state.
>
> (Milton and Rose Friedman, *Free to Choose*, Secker & Warburg, 1980)

This attitude of reducing welfare in the expectation that people will become self-reliant if there is no other option to them is similarly to be found in a North American welfare rights handbook:

> The government assures us that the Social Security system will never be allowed to fail, but it is possible that in 20 years benefits will be relatively lower than they are today. This means that if you can expect to receive less in the way of Social Security retirement benefits, you're going to have to assume greater personal responsibility for your future financial stability.
>
> (Getting the most from social security, *Consumer Guide Magazine*; vol. 446, no. 14, 1987)

do have very different ideas about its nature and scope. They believe that state support should not be monopolistic since that is unfair and inefficient; rather, welfare services should be provided by competing organisations in both the private and the public sectors. Public spending should be minimal, as should taxation, thereby creating incentives for people to initiate new enterprises and allow people more choice in how they would like to spend their money.

For many commentators, the expectation that social welfare should be provided in a competitive way by private organisations has highlighted the more general issue to be found in discussions of social policy of how far one can rely on private organisations, which are impelled by the profit motive, to meet individual and social needs. In health care, for example, expensive operations are more profitable than caring for the chronically sick and disabled or the mentally ill. If all hospitals were required to be profitable, therefore, there might be relatively few that would consider these unprofitable areas of care. This, in turn, has led to the argument that the policies of 'the New Right' have created a 'two-tier' system of caring; a comprehensive but expensive private system for those who can afford it (or have a job where health insurance is part of the 'occupational benefits' accruing to employees) and a reduced, minimal state system for everyone else.

Sociology, social policy and inequality

We have seen that there are differing notions of what is considered to be fair which are used to promote a particular set of policies and to justify the continued existence of inequalities, accompanied by ideas about the economy, need and so on. It is only with the Fabians that the pursuit of equality is a social policy goal, and even then it is gradual and piecemeal. Further, as **Alan Walker** points out, we must also look at the policy choices that governments reject to get a complete picture of the development of social policy in Britain. The choices that governments make may be influential in an intended or unintended way on the major inequalities in the British social structure of gender, race, class and generation.

Both *Ideology and Social Welfare* and *The Sociology of Welfare* include discussions of Marxism or Neo-Marxism as political ideologies. For the moment it is useful to keep the discussion to those ideologies which have had an influence on the actual development of social policy in Britain. Having seen that only the Fabians have held any kind of commitment to the goal of equality in any shape or form, one should not be surprised that all the evidence demonstrates that, in every aspect of social welfare and social policy, inequalities have persisted: in housing, education, health and, most of all, in income and wealth. In some areas, inequalities have actually increased since the development of what we know as the welfare state in 1948. George and Wilding suggest that this is because the predominant political ideology in Britain

Figure 3.4 **Capitalist values and social policy**
V. George and P. Wilding suggest that every society has a
dominant value system and they outline the dominant values
that support capitalism:

> Every economic system needs a legitimising ideology and
> capitalism is no exception. Such values as individualism,
> inequality, competition, private property are essential to
> a capitalist economic system and these values are gener-
> ally accepted and almost universally encouraged by
> societal institutions.
>
> V. George and P. Wilding, *Ideology and Social Welfare*,
> Routledge & Kegan Paul, rev. edn, 1985)

is liberalism. They argue that traditional liberal values such as
individual responsibility, support for the work ethic, competition
and so on are most suitable for the maintenance of capitalism. It
is likely, therefore, that it is this ideology that will be shaped and
developed by the powerful groups in capitalist societies who
have a vested interest in maintaining the status quo (see Figure
3.4).

Welfare ideologies – a critical discussion

This categorisation of political ideologies by George and Wilding,
Room, and others has been criticised in two principal ways. First,
Robert Pinker argues in *The Idea of Welfare* that George and
Wilding are mistaken in associating collectivism only with
socialism and by suggesting that Keynes and Beveridge were
'reluctant' in their attitude toward collectivism. Instead, Pinker
argues that they were 'enthusiastic collectivists' precisely because
they were not socialists. Further, he is critical of George and
Wilding for omitting what he considers to be a central aspect of
Marxist thought, the use of violence to achieve socialism. Pinker,
himself, has been criticised in making these observations since he
seems to be expressing his own value-laden preference for
retaining the eclectic and reformist social administration tradition
that many people now consider to be of limited use.

A second criticism levied against George and Wilding is that their work is *idealist* in seeking to advance an account of social policy which owes its force to what might be considered as 'rational' or 'reasonable'; that is, the only power that is mustered to support their particular socialist.conception of social policy is the force of argument. As **Lee** and **Raban** argue, they describe the various political ideologies without fully explaining why a particular set of values, those of liberalism in general, are predominant in British society – other than to say that they are the most suited to the maintenance of a capitalist society. In particular, they have been criticised for not examining popular conceptions of social policy and the welfare state. The views that politicians and academics hold of social policy and political values may differ widely from the views held by different, and much larger, groups in society – there are many more claimants than politicians and academics put together, and it is quite likely that their view of social welfare is quite different! What George and Wilding's analysis of political ideologies has omitted is a fully developed explanation of power in Britain, which perhaps helps to explain why considerations of gender, race and generation are given less attention in their analyses.

We are now in the unfortunate position of not knowing whose analysis to support since all the commentators seem to present their own views on what social policy should be within their respective analyses. What is needed is a more detailed explanation of the relationship between social policy, capitalism and inequality.

The social construction of social policy

Alan Walker argues that the failure to develop a fully social theory of social policy stems from the mistaken tradition of examining social policy and the welfare state as if they were synonymous, resulting in a view of welfare as something which is essentially reactive to problems rather than fully explaining their causes. Further, by identifying social policy with the welfare state, the only definition of need that is used is that provided by the state services themselves. This narrow view of need and social policy, argues Walker, is a result of its origins in the training of state workers, particularly social workers. This close association between the state services and the academics who studied them was further cemented by the latter's dependence on the state for research funding, course approval and so on; few researchers would want to bite the hand that feeds them.

Walker proposes an alternative perspective on social policy and social equality which has power as its central concept. This can be illustrated by examining the nature of income, wealth and poverty in Britain. There are a number of typical characteristics to the traditional study of poverty: (1) they describe who is poor, often using social surveys and the state's definition of poverty – eligibility for welfare benefits; (2) they describe what life is like for the poor, detailing the misery and hardship; (3) they may even describe the operation of the social security system and the meagreness of benefit payments; (4) they often describe the difficulties that many people have in claiming their entitlement, and the shame that claimants often are induced to feel about being poor; and (5) they identify a number of causes of poverty – low pay, unemployment, sickness, old age, separation and divorce.

The policy response from these analyses leads to arguments about definitions of poverty, the need to develop a notion of relative poverty, and a need to increase benefit and wage levels. They may also include a need to develop a simplified social security system – one which does not induce guilt, blame and shame. This .is, perhaps, an oversimplified view of traditional poverty studies and it would be wrong to dismiss them – they provide most useful empirical evidence on poverty and provoke discussions about new policies.

However, a critical analysis would extend this work further by asking, 'Why does poverty exist at all in our society, and why does it persist?'. In answering this question a critical analysis would examine the nature of power in capitalist societies, including the power relations of gender, race and generation, alongside discussions of social class – that is, it would ask, 'Who benefits from the continued existence of inequalities in income and wealth?' (see Figure 3.5). This, in turn, leads us to an analysis of economic policies and their effect on social policies. This can be illustrated by the recent discussions about 'social policies for work'. Unemployment in Britain started to rise appreciably in the 1970s with the onset of recession and the impact of the oil crisis. Following the election of the monetarist Conservative government in 1979 this rise was sharply accelerated as the government

Figure 3.5 **Inequalities in income**

A useful summary of differences in income and wealth is published in each edition of *Poverty*, the journal of the Child Poverty Action Group. The following facts and figures were all cited in *Poverty*, Spring 1986, no. 63:

A rich source of information about inequality in Britain is provided in 1984's Family Expenditure Survey.

EXPENDITURE

★ The 20% best-off households had an income nearly 10 times that of the 20% worst-off, and their expenditure was 5 times as high.

★ Britain's 20% poorest households spent a higher proportion of their incomes on basics such as heating and food:

– 13.04% of their expenditure went on fuel, compared to 4.31% spent by rich households;

– 28.7% of their weekly bill went on food, compared with 17.26% for the richest.

★ The wealthy spent only a little more each week on housing than the poor – 15.34% compared to 14.20%.

★ Average weekly household expenditure for a couple with two children excluding housing costs was £166.13.

★ SB rates for a similar family amounted to £64.75 – 39% of average expenditure.

In 1984 the best-off 20% of households received nearly half (49%) of all original income (i.e., income before direct government intervention through the tax and benefit system), while the worst-off 20% received 0.3%. Even taking into account all social security benefits, taxation and benefits such as health and education, the gap remains wide – the wealthiest 20% received 39% of final income, while the poorest received 7.1% after tax and benefits in cash and kind are included.

increased interest rates in order to curb inflation, making many firms unprofitable and unable to survive. At the start of 1979 the proportion of unemployed working people was 5.9 per cent. By the end of 1982 this had risen to nearly 13 per cent.

A number of studies of unemployment have consistently demonstrated that it has a dramatic effect in increasing people's social
needs. For example, **Dr Richard Smith**, assistant editor of the
British Medical Journal states in *Unemployment and Health* (Oxford
University Press, 1987) that unemployment kills at least 3 000
people a year. He goes on to say that 40 000 people will die
prematurely unless something is done about unemployment.
Stress was considered to be an important reason for these deaths.
According to **N. Beale** and **S. Nethercott**, even the threat of
redundancy can increase the level of illness ('Job loss and family
morbidity', *Journal of the Royal College of General Practitioners*,
Nov. 1984). Unemployment is both costly and harmful to unemployed people and acts as a brake on other welfare goals. As Alan
Walker concludes:

> Without a positive policy to reduce unemployment all of the
> other progressive objectives of social policy are called into
> question, not least by the demands on resources to pay even
> basic subsistence benefits. In other words, without an employ-
> ment policy the future for welfare is very bleak indeed.
>
> (A. Walker, 'Sharing the job shortage', in R. Klein and M.
> O'Higgins (eds), *The Future of Welfare*, Basil Blackwell,
> 1985)

What this discussion illustrates is that to understand the causes of
contemporary poverty we must examine the economic policies
that were created to support the continued profitability of British
enterprise. The gap between the rich and the poor has actually
increased since 1979, as the rich have increased their wealth as a
consequence of government policies. Further, the effects of these
policies have not only been detrimental to the unemployed, they
have also reduced resources for more general spending on social
welfare. Whatever policies we may design to deal with poverty,
the roots of inequalities in income are to be found in the sphere
of work and production – as the slogan of the International
Women's Garment Workers Union in the USA more succinctly
puts it: *'We don't want welfare, we want work'*.

In conclusion, then, whatever definition of equality we may
use, the fact remains that few policies have actually sought to
create a more equal society. Further, our explanation of the
continued existence of social inequalities in Britain must locate
social policies in the wider context of the continued reproduction

Figure 3.6 **Inequalities in wealth**
Dominic Byrne demonstrates that the gap between the rich and the poor is widening:

Since 1979 the gap between the high paid and the low paid has widened into a huge gulf. So much so that the poorest workers are now markedly more worse off compared to higher earners than they were 100 years ago when pay statistics were first gathered:

★ in 1986 manual workers in the bottom fifth of the pay ladder received 69% of the average male manual wage;
★ in 1986 wages in the bottom fifth of the manual distribution were worth only 65% of the average;
★ over the same period the top fifth in the manual pay league have moved upwards – from 43% above the average to 55% above.

The trends identified in earnings, taxes and benefits are reflected in patterns of income and wealth distribution. Until the late 1970s there had been a long-term trend towards a marginal redistribution of wealth. However, this historical trend was from the very rich to the rich, rather from rich to poor. Redistribution since the inter-war period failed to reach much beyond the top 20%. During the Thatcher years, however, even that small amount of redistribution has been halted. The clear effect of current government policy has been to buttress existing extremes of wealth. In 1984:

★ over half (52%) of all personal marketable wealth was owned by the richest 10%;
★ more than a fifth (21%) of personal marketable wealth was concentrated in the hands of the richest 1%;
★ in stark contrast, the bottom 50% of the population controlled just 7% of marketable wealth.
(Dominic Byrne, 'Rich and poor: the growing divide', in Alan Walker and Carol Walker (eds), *The Growing Divide – a Social Audit 1979–1987*, CPAG Ltd, 1987)

of capitalism and the power relationships that are implicit in capitalist societies. On those occasions when equality has been an issue it has tended to be exceptional rather than a part of an overall strategy and, typically, 'equality of opportunity' or 'equal access' has been the notion of fairness used rather than the more radical 'equality of outcome' (see Figure 3.6).

4 The welfare state

The traditional view of the British welfare state is one which sees its development as gradual and evolutionary. Such a view tends to take the principal areas of education, health, housing, income maintenance and personal social services and describe the history of their respective policies as though there was a steady improvement in service provision. This corresponds to the liberal social administration tradition with its focus on individuals, rather than groups, and its concern with pragmatism, rather than with theoretical analysis. For the sociologist, the history of the welfare state is an important element of analysis but not, in itself, sufficient to explain fully the development of the welfare state.

According to **David Marsh**, it was not until the late 1930s that the term 'welfare state' was coined:

> probably by the internationally known Oxford scholar Alfred Zimmern, who used it to point out the contrast with the Power State of the Fascist dictators. The term is first found in print, in this sense, in Archbishop William Temple's book of 1941 *Citizen and Churchman* and was soon to be given wider connotation and circulation in Britain by the Beveridge Report of 1942.
>
> (D. C. Marsh, *The Welfare State*, Longman, 1970, 2nd edn, 1980)

Marsh suggests that the date when the modern welfare state in Britain came into existence might be taken as 5 July 1948, when the schemes for National Insurance, National Assistance and the National Health Service came into force.

In attempting to explain the development of the welfare state a number of influences might be traced, although, at the outset, there were many people who were opposed to the extension of state powers over the lives of individuals, preferring the traditions of self-help and voluntary help as ways of coping with need. Nevertheless, a number of factors are usually cited to explain the creation of the welfare state in 1948.

1 The Poor Law tradition: From the Elizabethan Poor Laws onwards – there had been a recognition that some help must be afforded to the poor and needy; not only to satisfy their needs but also to satisfy a need for social order. From the sixteenth century through to the present the poor have been seen to pose a potential threat to the established social order. In 1834 this led to the passing of the Poor Law Amendment Act which committed all claimants to the workhouse with its deliberate ethos of harshness and brutality. (The introduction of the workhouse was opposed in many areas by working-class groups and by the middle-class 'visitors of the poor').

2 Throughout the nineteenth century ideas changed about the role of state intervention. The *laissez-faire* ethos at the beginning of the century was gradually replaced by support for the state assuming some responsibility for people's lives. Powerful groups were mindful of the revolution and general unrest that could be seen in other countries, and social reform seemed to be one way in which social unrest in Britain might be obviated. By the end of the century the labour movement had grown, as had the intellectual force of Fabianism, and state intervention was widely supported.

3 The role of individuals: As rapid industrialism generated an increase in problems so a number of influential individuals sought to pass reforms to improve living and working conditions, particularly in the growing industrial towns and cities. Such individuals as Octavia Hill and Edwin Chadwick in the nineteenth century and Beveridge and Bevan in the twentienth century make up a list of reforming and campaigning people whose work demonstrated the need for a welfare state. However, we would be mistaken if we explained the development of the welfare state as a series of individual achievements; rather, we must examine the social, political and economic contexts within which these individuals worked.

4 The surveys of poverty by people such as Booth, Rowntree and Mayhew demonstrated that the poor could not be held responsible for their poverty. Similarly, reports on the health of working-class people, on their living conditions and so on, accompanied by the collapse of the workhouse system through overcrowding, led to a recognition that the state ought to intervene with a new strategy for meeting need.

Figure 4.1 **The development of the welfare state**
Pat Thane describes in detail how other countries developed
social policies which were subsequently introduced in
Britain. She argues that most industrialised countries were
experiencing similar problems towards the end of the nineteenth century; problems of poverty, ill health, poor housing
and so on. She also distinguishes between imperialist countries which faced these problems and 'immigrant countries'
such as New Zealand, Australia and the western United
States, where the population tended to be younger and there
was land to spare.

Of the imperialist countries, Germany was the first to
make significant provision of a new kind for her own
citizens. In 1884 Bismarck, Chancellor of Germany,
introduced the first system in the world of compulsory
national insurance against sickness. All regularly employed
German workers thereafter paid weekly contributions,
graduated according to income, into a national fund, and
received weekly benefits and health care when needed.
. . . State supported old-age pensions were indeed among
the first state measures to be introduced in many countries. Denmark in 1891 introduced non-contributory old-
age pensions for those over sixty-five who could prove
destitution, through a means test. Similar schemes were
introduced by each of the Australian states from 1900,
and by New Zealand in 1898. France introduced pensions
for miners and railwaymen in the 1890s.
(Pat Thane, *The Foundations of the Welfare State*
Longman, 1982).

5 In considering a new strategy, Britain was able to look at the
new schemes developed in other countries, particularly in
Germany and New Zealand (see Figure 4.1).

6 By the end of the nineteenth century Britain's economic world
supremacy and development were vulnerable to increased competition in international trade, particularly from Germany, the

United States and France, whose economies were growing at the same time as the British economy started to decline.

7 The culmination of these forces can be seen in the Liberal reforms of 1900 to 1914, especially the Old Age Pensions Act of 1908 and the National Insurance Act of 1911, which introduced the insurance principle into British social security legislation, although relatively few people were covered and the amounts they would receive were low. It would be mistaken, however, to consider these policies as the creation of a welfare state. Writing to his secretary, Lloyd George makes clear that that was not his intention:

> Insurance necessarily temporary expedient. At no distant date hope state will acknowledge full responsibility in the matter of making provision for sickness, breakdown and unemployment.
> (Cited by Asa Briggs, 'Towards the welfare state', in P. Barker (ed.), *Founders of the Welfare State*, Heinemann Educational Books, 1984)

8 Most commentators argue that the two world wars made a significant contribution to the move towards a welfare state. During both wars the state assumed greater responsibility for the welfare of the population. Women were able to enter the workplace and undertake jobs which had been denied them beforehand. However, they were expected to return to the home after each war was over. Women had a significant influence on the proposals for new welfare policies. In both wars governments argued that there would be reforms after the war; the population was promised a 'land fit for heroes' after the First World War; and the Beveridge Plan for social insurance was published during the Second World War. The 1920s and 1930s were a period of economic depression and high unemployment, and the inadequacies of the existing system of National Insurance became clear as unemployed people quickly used up their entitlement and were once more dependent on the national means-tested system of assistance. (A means-tested benefit is one where all your income, and in some cases your assets such as savings, are taken into account before you may be entitled to basic support; see Figure 4.2.)

The response to all of these influences culminated in the Beveridge Report; properly known as the Report on Social Insurance and

Figure 4.2 **The impact of the Second World War**
Titmuss argued that the Second World War had a major
influence on the development of social policy and the welfare
state, as summarised by Tony Cole:

> 1 Popular opinion was affected by the shared vulner-
> ability of war and social solidarity was enhanced by
> opposition to a common enemy. This reduced many
> people's opposition to egalitarian and collectivist policies.
> 2 As middle class families in country areas took in poor
> and working class children evacuated from the bombed
> cities, there was a spread of information about the degree
> of poverty and general nature of social problems.
> 3 The government was willing to respond to these
> because it wanted a fit, nourished, efficient and contented
> nation.
>
> (Tony Cole, *Whose Welfare?* Tavistock Publications,
> 1986)

Allied Services, it was published in 1942 and was an immediate
'best-seller' and gained wide support from politicians, trade
unions and so on. It proposed to get rid of the five giant social
evils of Squalor, Disease, Ignorance, Idleness and Want by
extending the principle of National Insurance so that everyone
would be secure 'from cradle to grave'. In addition to a universal
system of social security it also proposed the introduction of a
universal, comprehensive and free National Health Service. There
was to be a system of National Assistance providing minimal
means-tested support for those people who initially fell through
the 'welfare net', although it was thought that the need for
National Assistance would diminish. Alongside these proposals
we must also situate the Butler Education Act of 1944 which
extended state education so that all children would receive a free
secondary education.

The post-war welfare state, 1951–79

By 1950 Britain had the fastest growing system of social welfare in the world. From the outset, however, the welfare state had its critics. The 1945–51 Labour government was committed to expanding social welfare; the Housing Act of 1949, for example, extended the subsidies available for building council houses. The principle informing this administration was that of *universalism* – that is, social welfare was to be available for all, paid for by all. By 1952 right-wing commentators and politicians were questioning the whole basis of social welfare, arguing that it could not be afforded. From the Left came the criticism that the system of social security was not sufficiently comprehensive; benefit levels were too low and too many people fell through the insurance net; instead they called for a more generous system of *earnings-related* benefits.

The Conservative government of 1951–64 presided over a period of economic growth – the 'Golden Fifties'. House-building boomed and people talked of an end to inequality. Despite the earlier criticisms the government did not dismantle the welfare state, although there were few policy innovations in this period. When Labour were returned to office in 1964 they were conscious of the rediscovery of poverty and social need but were split on whether to expand universalist services or pursue more selectivist ones where only some, particularly needy, groups benefited from social provision. The selectivists won and prescription charges, for example, were introduced in January 1968. This debate was further complicated by the introduction of new ideas about positive discrimination which maintained that, rather than pursue policies of equality which had limited efficacy, *equitable* policies should be pursued which provided support for those in greater need. Positive discrimination was introduced in education following the Plowden Report of 1967, creating Educational Priority Areas in 'run-down' urban areas. Similarly, Community Development Projects and Urban Aid programmes were developed to give extra support to needy areas.

By the late 1960s the economic growth of the 1950s had swung to a period of decline. The Conservative government elected in 1970 under Edward Heath embraced selectivism as a means of reducing public expenditure and taxes; means-testing was extended, particularly in social security. The Labour government of 1974–79 faced a growing inflation rate, increasing unemployment, a high level of public spending and pressure from the International Monetary Fund, and continued, therefore, to support selective social provision. Overall, the period 1951–79 saw Conservative and Labour governments differ markedly with regard to policies but share a consensus on a commitment to public provision through a welfare state. In housing, for example, Labour governments favoured extending public provision whilst Conservative governments promoted owner-occupation. Even though it was a Conservative minister, Edward Boyle, who laid much of the foundation for comprehensive education, Conservatives have favoured selective education and private education, whereas Labour politicians have been committed to the development of comprehensive education and a dimunition of fee-paying education. Both parties have supported the National Health Service although they differ on private health schemes – Labour wishing to remove them and Conservatives promoting them. However, by 1979 this shared commitment to the principle of a welfare state ended with the election of a monetarist Conservative government, which pledged to cut back the nature and scope of state welfare and to replace it by services provided by the private sector.

The effectiveness of the welfare state

Notwithstanding the continued election of right-wing Conservative governments committed to reducing welfare state provision, most people support the existence of a welfare state; perhaps highlighting the National Health Service or state schooling as illustrations of how important these services are. However, we must scrutinise the achievements of the welfare state carefully if uncritical support for state welfare is to be sustained.

The aims of the welfare state

In order to measure the success of the welfare state it is important to ascertain what it set out to do. We have already seen that the goal of equality has had a limited influence on social policies. Instead, we might consider the success of the welfare state in meeting the aims it sets for itself. David Marsh clearly states what he considers these aims to be:

If, for example, one looks at the Scandinavian countries, or New Zealand, Australia or Britain, then it seems as though they all attempt: (a) to ensure the maintenance of employment so as to guarantee the right to live for most of us; (b) to ensure the maintenance of a minimum income at all times; (c) to ensure the right to learn; and (d) the right to protection and community support when one is incapacitated physically or mentally.

> (D. C. Marsh, *The Welfare State*, Longman, 1970, 2nd edn, 1980)

Vic George and **Paul Wilding** in *The Impact of Social Policy* are more equivocal about identifying the aims of the welfare state and social policy:

> The aims of social policy are what social policies intend or hope to achieve. Inevitably, there is disagreement among different groups in society about the aims of social policy. Thus the view of the Conservative Government , on the Industrial Relations Act, 1971, was that its aim was to restore industrial peace and hence improve the economic position of all groups in society. The view of the trades unions was that the aim of the legislation was to curb their activities, reduce their power and hence lower the economic position of their members vis-à-vis that of the employers.
>
> (V. George and P. Wilding, *The Impact of Social Policy*, Routledge & Kegan Paul, 1984)

They also point out that there may be unintended or unanticipated aims and consequences of social policy. The Children and Young Persons Act, 1969, for example, was intended to keep young people out of the criminal justice system but resulted in more young people entering the system than ever before. As they conclude:

> Any verdict on the real aims of social policy is essentially a matter of interpretation and value-judgement.
>
> (Ibid.)

In *The Impact of Social Policy* they state that the 'most generally agreed aim' of social policy since 1945 has been the 'achievement of socially acceptable minimum standards' since minimum standards, rather than notions of equality or equity, do not challenge the liberal–democratic values which underpin capitalism; indeed, minimum standards in welfare can be seen to support capitalism by encouraging competition, providing incentives and ameliorating the worst extremes of hardship that might provide the basis for conflict. In order to evaluate the success of the welfare state in meeting its intended aims we may consider the achievement of minimum standards in the main areas of welfare state provision. It must be recognised, however, that most of these discussions only consider the *institutional responses* to social needs and exclude, for example, the role of the family, of employers and trade unions, of voluntary organisations and so on in meeting needs.

Incomes

We saw in the previous chapter that inequalities in income have widened, but what of minimum incomes? Taking the commonly used definition of poverty, that of eligibility for social security benefits, which is a most meagre definition, a number of observations have been made: (1) the social security system does give minimal support to most people in need who live below the official poverty line; however, (2) the number of claimants has dramatically increased since 1979, and (3) in 1984 almost 3 million people had incomes *below* that level; (4) the old, the low-waged, single parents (most of whom are single mothers), the sick and disabled, and the unemployed are most likely to have incomes below benefit levels; (5) the real value of benefits has dropped; (6) many people do not claim the benefits to which they are entitled, and (7) for many people, a small increase in their wages or reduction in tax threshold means that they lose entitlement and are actually worse off as a result (the *poverty trap*).

> In 1983 estimates for the take-up of benefits showed that 1 290 000 people were not receiving the benefit to which they were entitled, saving the government £570 million per year. Pensioners had the lowest take-up rate of 67%. The average amount of unclaimed benefit was £8.40 per week but for the unemployed it was £15.90.
> (*Poverty*, Winter 1986/87, no. 65)

In addition, we must consider new types of poverty that have become apparent in the 1980s. For example, most welfare rights organisations have expressed concern about the rising incidence of personal debt, including fuel debts which lead to disconnection; and housing debts which lead to eviction and the repossession of houses by building societies and banks. Similarly, *rural poverty* has risen in recent years. Agricultural workers have always been amongst the lowest paid, but following government policies over the last ten years it has become more expensive to live in rural areas with the closure of village schools, the reduction in transport facilities and the removal of post offices, telephone boxes and the migration of doctors away from rural practices.

Health

It is more difficult to identify minimum standards in health, where the achievement of optimum standards has been the aim and where many of the causes of ill-health are to be found outside the purview of the National Health Service. As the White Paper of 1944 which preceded the establishment of the NHS states, the aim is to ensure that 'in future every man, woman and child can rely on getting all the advice, treatment and care which they may need in matters of personal health'.

Despite continued growth in the size and budget of health services, it is clear that this aim has not been achieved. Undoubtedly, many of the 'killer diseases' of the past such as cholera and typhus have been largely eradicated, but the evidence suggests that these 'diseases of poverty' have been diminished as a result of better diet, better housing, pure water and better environments generally. In turn, they have been replaced by the 'diseases of affluence', notably cancers and heart complaints. Further, inequalities that existed prior to the establishment of the NHS have largely persisted, and in some cases increased – inequalities of gender, social class, race, age and geographical area. Such is the difficulty in meeting health needs that some commentators have suggested that the NHS is on the verge of collapse in some areas (see Figure 4.3).

Housing

The aim of housing policies and a statement of minimum standards is also debatable. George and Wilding suggest that the aim can be inferred from post-war housing policies:

Figure 4.3 **Crisis in the NHS**

In February 1980, in Liverpool, a 92 year old spinster died alone at home after a warning that she did not expect to survive being discharged from hospital. The senior consultant defended his decision to send her home by saying that he was under pressure to cut the number of old people's beds. In Durham, one hospital has decided to switch off the heating at night to save money, and only the intensive care and maternity units are excepted. In Enfield, North London, patients have been stranded in an upstairs ward for three years because the lifts are broken and the Area Health Authority claims to have no money to install new ones. According to the Consultant Physician, 48 geriatric patients are not receiving adequate treatment.

In 1979, a doctor in Hackney was quoted as saying, 'We have real problems getting emergency admissions into hospital, even people with miscarriages and suspected heart attacks. I sometimes have to phone three or four hospitals to find them a bed and then it's often miles from their home'.

(CIS, *NHS – Critical Condition*, Counter Information Services, undated)

The minimum aims of government housing policies have been the provision of enough dwellings of an acceptable standard and density for all households and at a price within the financial means of each household.

(V. George and P. Wilding, *The Impact of Social Policy*, Routledge & Kegan Paul, 1984).

Since 1951, the number of houses has grown faster than the number of households, and by 1980 there were over 1 million more houses than households. If there was an equitable distribution of houses, therefore, housing policies may be considered to have met their aims. However, not all of the available houses are fit to live in. The English House Condition Survey in 1981 showed that 1.2 million houses were unfit for habitation, although about 1 million were actually occupied. Further, a Department of the Environment inquiry into local authority housing in 1985 revealed that approximately 84 per cent of dwellings were reported in need of some sort of repair. The number of homeless people has actually increased. That is, although there is an excess of dwellings over households, many of these are second homes, many are unsuitable or unfit, and many are too expensive for most people. The evidence suggests that the aim of housing policy to secure a decent home for everyone is less likely to be met now than in the past. Further, although there has been a trend towards home ownership in recent years, so there has been an increase in the number of houses repossessed. In 1979 building societies repossessed approximately 2500 properties. In 1985 this figure had grown to approximately 16 800.

Education

For more than ten years governments have expressed concern about standards in education. The 'great debate' launched in the 1970s about teaching standards and the curriculum still continues, with the introduction of a 'core curriculum', more assessment of pupils and closer appraisal of teachers. But what is the evidence on standards in education? George and Wilding suggest that, even though there has been a decline in the standards of school buildings, support services, and equipment and books, the standards measured in terms of class size, teacher expertise and literacy have all improved since 1944. For example, 67 per cent of primary school classes had over thirty pupils in them in 1950, compared with 28.5 per cent in 1979 and 18.6 in 1985. (The figure for 1985 was higher than the figure for 1984, but it is too soon to ascertain whether government education policies have caused a reversal in this general trend.)

What is clear is that an increasing number of parents are not satisfied with state education since the number of children entering private education has increased. In recent years there has been concern about the standard of teaching, yet all teachers are now professionally trained and the duration of training is longer than in 1944. Perhaps, as George and Wilding suggest, debates about teachers are often 'ideological and political' rather than 'scientific and technical'. What is clear from the evidence is that, although there has been some diminution in educational in-

Figure 4.4
Inge Bates *et al.* argue that education policies have had little effect on social inequality.

> Studies of trends in education have shown the following:
> a) a general increase in the levels of educational attainment;
> b) this trend has been most pronounced for lower class groups;
> c) consequently there has been a progressive reduction in educational inequality in attainment;
> d) but this has not been associated with a corresponding reduction in *social* inequalities, for example, in increased social mobility, narrowing of income differentials;
> e) this is because this trend is internally associated with credential inflation in the labour market. People in general, and lower class groups in particular, require successively higher levels of attainment simply in order to maintain existing status.
> f) through time, given levels of educational attainment and their associated educational career paths are corresponding to successively lower occupational categories. For this reason, educational career paths cannot be treated as agencies of identity formation, socialising pupils into predestined occupational positions, because there is no enduring relationship between particular career paths and particular occupational positions.
>
> (Inge Bates, John Clarke, Philip Cohen, Dann Finn, Robert Moore and Paul Willis, *Schooling for the Dole? the New Vocationalism*, Macmillan, 1984)

equalities, the changes in education policy have had little effect on the wider inequalities in the social structure (see Figure 4.4).

Personal social services

By personal social services is meant a range of services such as home helps, residential care for the elderly or the disabled, provision of health visitors, social workers and so on. Despite growth and consolidation in these services since 1945 by most, if not all, criteria of minimum standards, it is difficult to find a major success story. That is, there are large numbers of people who do not get the support they need.

Currently, the principle of *community care* is popular whereby needy people are cared for in the community, usually in their own homes. Some commentators, however, see this simply as a means of reducing social services expenditure. George and Wilding point out, for example, that economic recession and the election of a Conservative government committed to reducing public expenditure has 'meant the abandonment of national guidelines for the social services'.

Conclusion

This scrutiny of the minimal standards achieved by the welfare state may be considered by some to concentrate too much on the 'doom and gloom' aspects of the welfare state without doing justice to the achievements. Overall, there are better educated people living in better dwellings who may receive medical and health care as of right who would not enjoy those services but for the welfare state. Nevertheless, a review of minimal standards does indicate that the welfare state has not yet met most of its aims.

Further, in examining in more detail these gaps in welfare provision what also becomes clear are the real inequalities that exist in welfare provision. Not only do middle-class people benefit more from the welfare state than working-class people, but women, black people and older people all experience the welfare state as one of the principal agencies that discriminate against them in society. That is, the welfare state does not, primarily, support those in greatest need. Instead, those with high levels of need are most likely to experience the welfare state as a source of repression and control rather than as a source of help.

5 Theories of the welfare state

In order to develop a fully social theory of the welfare state we must extend our analysis further than a description of the welfare state's development, its principal aims and its successes and failures; that is, an examination of sociological theories is required to explain the nature and scope of the welfare state.

Industrialisation and the welfare state

The development of a welfare state seems to be a concomitant of industrial development; however, we may be critical of those analyses, such as *convergence theories* and theories proposing some form of *technological determinism* which suggest that the welfare state is an inevitable part of industrial development. First, these theories fail to develop any satisfactory explanation for this apparent inevitability. Second, they fail to recognise the nature and extent of social conflict in industrial societies, including conflict in social policy. They do not account for the possibility of reversal in social policy, let alone the attempts in the 1980s to reduce considerably the welfare state's activities.

Functionalism and the welfare state

The modern welfare state did not exist at the time the early functionalists, such as Spencer and Durkheim, were developing their sociological theories. Nevertheless, they did consider social policy, indirectly, in their work. **R. Mishra** states that Spencer was opposed to state intervention, although his arguments were polemical rather than sociological and do not contribute much to the analysis of welfare. Durkheim, on the other hand, believed that social regulation was important as a means of securing social solidarity and social order in complex, organic societies. Durkheim's ideas can be seen to have influenced later functionalists, such as Parsons and Smelser, working in the USA.

Gouldner points out in *The Coming Crisis in Western Sociology* (Heinemann Educational Books, 1970) that functionalism initially had an ambivalent attitude towards welfare, recognising, on the one hand, that the state had a role in finding solutions to social problems, and, on the other hand, that they were concerned that centralised planning would undermine what they believed to be the natural development of moral consensus in society. According to Gouldner, it was after the Second World War that function-alism in the USA gave explicit support to the welfare state as a means of regulating the economy and protecting society from the threat of communism. For functionalists, the welfare state replaces religious organisations in complex industrial societies as the insti-tution which serves to secure integration and harmony in the community.

Mishra is critical of the functionalist view of welfare, arguing that it is one-sided. We must remember that social policies may have intended or unintended consequences that favour one group but not everyone in society. Merton did recognise that some policy consequences may be 'dysfunctional', but to admit such a thing is to permit conflict to enter the analysis and coercion as a means of dealing with it. This stands in contrast to the func-tionalist assumption that societies are self-regulating. If we examine the unintended consequences in detail, such as the stigma which is attached to an area because of selective council dwell-ing allocation policies, it becomes clear that the welfare state is central to an analysis of conflict and control – something which lies outside the scope of functionalist analysis. Finally, function-alism claims to be universal in its analysis; however, the diversity between different welfare states in countries with similar social and economic development demonstrates the sterility of this analysis of welfare. As Mishra concludes:

> In recent years, the fortunes of functionalism as a social theory have declined precipitously. The rediscovery of poverty, privi-lege and exploitation in the United States and elsewhere in the West, the problems of racism and sexism, the relations between the advanced and the Third World, the difficulties of the capi-talist economy in the 1970s have all in different ways undermined the credibility of a doctrine based on the notions of harmony, equilibrium and value-consensus.
>
> (R. Mishra, *Society and Social Policy*, Macmillan, 1977, 2nd edn, 1981)

Marxism and the welfare state

Marxist theories of the welfare state offer a number of important insights into the nature and scope of state welfare. First, Marxists have drawn attention to the role of class conflict in securing welfare reforms. Marx himself saw working-class support for the Factory Acts in nineteenth-century Britain as an illustration of how working-class action could lead to immediate, albeit piece-meal, positive gains. As **Paul Corrigan** states:

> The major political force to be understood in terms of welfare provision is the working class. At all stages the working-class struggle has had some form of effect upon the provision of welfare in the UK.
>
> (Paul Corrigan, 'The welfare state as an arena of class struggle', *Marxism Today*, March 1977)

Corrigan cites the rent strike in Glasgow during the First World War as an illustration of the point that welfare achievements were not necessarily granted by a beneficent state, but were fought for through working-class struggle. In recent years Marxist analysis has developed the central ideas of *political economy* in the field of social welfare; that is, Marxists have examined the role of the welfare state in securing the continuation of a capitalist economic system (see Figure 5.1).

For Marxists, the welfare state is a contested terrain with different class interests competing for social policies which support their respective interests. In considering this 'dual nature' of the welfare state it must also be remembered that the different social classes are not seen to meet as equals in the contest over social policy. Further, since the interests of capital are likely to dominate in the state, then policies which appear to be initially quite radical may well lose that radical content and even be reversed through the processes of amendment and implementation. Corrigan cites the 1965 Rent Act, which was supposed to have extended rent controls but, in practice, led to more rents being increased than decreased.

Finally, Marxists have also drawn attention to the ways in which influences which lie outside social policy and the welfare state may still have an important bearing on whether a policy will be successful. For example, the productivity of the building industry may affect the prices of new schools, hospitals and

Figure 5.1 **Capitalism and the welfare state**
Central to discussions of the relationship between capitalism
and welfare have been O'Connor's *The Fiscal Crisis of the
State* (St Martin's Press, 1973) and I. Gough's *The Political
Economy of the Welfare State* (Macmillan Press, 1979).

Three important elements in the relationship between
capitalism and the welfare state are identified in analysing
the way the welfare state helps to sustain capitalism; *accumu-
lation, reproduction*, and *legitimation/repression*. That is, the
welfare state ensures that there is a healthy and suitably
educated workforce (inculcated with the appropiate values
in support of the work ethic). The welfare state also
provides a means of securing support for the existing socio-
economic structure by creating the appearance of satisfying
needs and providing opportunites for individual achievement. These aspects of the welfare state are contradictory
in that the aspirations of people fostered by the welfare state
cannot be met by a production system which relies on the
exploitation of working people in order to exist.

There is a danger, however, that this analysis becomes
economistic; that is, that everything is explained solely in
terms of the economic needs of capital. The recognition that
class conflict is an integral part of the development of the
welfare state prevents us from seeing the later as nothing
more than a conspiracy of the 'ruling class' who are never
identified and whose activities are forever clandestine. For
example, monetarist economic policies have led to greater
unemployment so that industry can remain profitable;
however, this has led to a concomitant increase in social
security spending. With reductions in social security
payments dissatisfaction may be engendered which requires
money to be spent on social control activities. There is now
some evidence, for example, that there is an increase in petty
crime accompanying the increase in unemployment: more
police are recruited, the prisons become more overcrowded,
insurance premiums increase and so on. The *legitimacy* of
government is threatened, so money has to be spent on reinforcing the work ethic. For example, claimants who 'seem'
to have given up trying to find a job may be required to
attend a rehabilitation centre to 'remind' them of what work
is like.

houses. Further, builders may find that they can make more money building houses for the private market rather than for the local authority, so that even if the money was available there would be difficulty in building the houses. In some local authorities there are now shortages of skilled workers such as bricklayers, plasterers, plumbers and so on because those people can make more money doing subcontracted work than working for a local authority.

Notwithstanding the important contributions that Marxists have made to the analysis of the welfare state, a number of criticisms need to be made. First, Marxist analyses have an uneasy view of the state. On the one hand, state action in capitalist society is viewed as one of the ways in which the powerful classes secure the continuation of a capitalist economic system. On the other hand, the analyses imply that the welfare state should be fought for and any spending cuts should be resisted. Obviously, this is a simplified criticism, and Marxists have addressed the question themselves (see, for example, The London Edinburgh Weekend Return Group, *In and Against the State*, Pluto Press 1979.) However, the precise relationship between class and the welfare state is still unclear. This confusion may be a consequence of Marx himself viewing welfare development as an alternative to capitalist development, yet all the evidence shows that a high level of collective provision is possible without any threat to capitalism.

Second, we cannot fully support the explanation which views the welfare state solely as a contested ideological state apparatus in the service of capital since, as Mishra points out, many of the criticisms of the controlling nature of the welfare state in capitalist societies can also be applied to systems of welfare in socialist societies.

Third, issues of gender, race and generation are often excluded from Marxist analyses and where they do appear, they are often subsumed under the heading of class, thereby failing to recognise the distinctive dimensions of sex, race and age discrimination.

Marxist analyses have contributed considerably to the development of more valid and critical explanation of the nature and development of the welfare state in capitalist societies; however, because they have overlooked many of the important aspects of the welfare state we have to look elsewhere to get a more complete picture.

Feminists and the welfare state

One way of looking at social policy would be to describe it as a set of structures created by men to shape the lives of women.

(E. Wilson, 'Feminism and social policy', in M. Loney, D. Boswell and J. Clarke (eds), *Social Policy and Social Welfare*, Open University Press, 1983)

Feminist analyses of the welfare state provide us with a powerful critique, not only of the welfare state, but also of the way in which it has been studied. As a result we must question many of the taken-for-granted assumptions about social policy.

Terminology

Dale Spender, in *Man Made Language* (Routledge & Kegan Paul, 1980), argues that not only have men formulated a language to suit their own needs, they have also maintained a monopolistic control over language, and in so doing, they constantly reaffirm patriarchal control over women. In *Social Policy – a Feminist Analysis*, **Gill Pascall** points out that terms such as 'unemployment' and 'one-parent family' conceal a reality in social policy that is not recognised in most discussions of the welfare state.

Unemployment belongs to a male working life rather than a female one. . . .

[One-parent families] suggests that single motherhood and single fatherhood can be lumped together.

(G. Pascall, *Social Policy – a Feminist Analysis*, Tavistock, 1986)

A further terminological consideration is that of 'household', and **Mary McIntosh** in 'The state and the oppression of women' (in A. Kuhn and A. M. Wolpe (eds), *Feminism and Materialism*, Routledge & Kegan Paul, 1978) describes how the capitalist state prescribes living in a 'household', which is then treated as if it were a single unit. Social security entitlement, for example, is based on an income entering a 'household'; yet, as **Jan Pahl**'s research has demonstrated, there is no guarantee that an income earned by a man will be equitably distributed to other members of the 'household' according to their needs. This applies to married people and cohabiting people alike.

The assumption that the household is a single unit gives power to the main income earner, who is usually the man, since men's wages are still, on average, higher than women's, supported by such notions as 'a family wage' or 'a living wage'. That is, men, through trade unions and in other ways have argued that they need an income to support themselves and 'their' families, even though there is no guarantee that the money will go to their families. Treating the household as a single unit is one of the ways in which dependency on a man by women and children is fostered by social policy. The other side of this coin is the fact that responsibility for budgeting, feeding and clothing the children and so on usually falls to the mother. In other words, the person with the greatest need to have, and control, the household income is often the person who is least likely to be in a position to do so.

Feminists have also been critical of the language of 'community care'. It is argued that 'community care' offers a better alternative to institutions for the satisfaction of needs. Feminists have argued that 'community care' is euphemistic for the unpaid work that women do in the family.

Origins of welfare

A feminist analysis not only requires us to think again about the terms we use, but it also requires us to look again at the development of the welfare state. We have seen how the evolutionary or functionalist view cannot be sustained, but have noted the useful insights to be gained from a Marxist analysis. However, a number of feminist writers, such as **Olive Banks**, have demonstrated that we need to reappraise the history of the welfare state in the light of the evidence that women were extremely influential in campaigning for policy reforms. Many groups of women worked within the labour movement to secure reforms, and to see positive policy gains solely in terms of class struggle is mistaken.

> In the years immediately before the first world war they ran influential campaigns for equal divorce laws for men and women, for better maternity and infant welfare and for maternity benefits to be paid to mothers.
> (O. Banks, *Faces of Feminism*, Martin Robertson, 1981)

Similarly, Banks describes the Women's Labour League, which

was founded in 1906 and campaigned for such things as 'school meals, medical inspections in schools, the provision of nursery schools, and pit-head baths' (ibid.).

Not all of the groups shared the same aims, however, and there were important differences that are still important. Perhaps one of the most pertinent of these is whether to campaign for equality with men in all spheres of social life – such as work and politics – as well as demand equality in the home; or whether to campaign for the revaluing and granting of due support for women working in the home. One of the principal protagonists of the latter view was Eleanor Rathbone, who fought for a 'family endowment' scheme to pay an income to mothers, thereby according a proper value to the work women do in the home at the same time as giving them some independence from their husbands. This is echoed today in the 'Wages for Housework' campaign. Critics have argued, however, that this does not radically change anything, since it affirms the belief that the woman's role is to care for others in the family. This was reflected in the Beveridge Report, for example, which introduced children's allowances, but was seen as an attempt to encourage couples to have more children; indeed, an amendment had to be forced to get payment made direct to mothers rather than payment to fathers. Perhaps this illustrates the ambivalence shown by the Labour Party and trade unions in fully supporting women's attempts at gaining equality.

Feminist explanations of the welfare state

Gill Pascall argues that, since there are a variety of feminist approaches, there is 'no single feminist social policy'. Further, she contends that feminist approaches to welfare appear to be contradictory. On the one hand, the welfare state can be seen to control women's lives and reproduce an ideology that confines women to caring for others in the home; on the other hand, the welfare state has been seen to be supportive of women, and, as we have seen, development of the welfare state was a central concern of feminists in the past.

One of the central concerns of a feminist analysis is that of *reproduction* in capitalist society, and feminists have been critical of the political economy approach developed by Marxists, with its concentration on the role of *production* in capitalist society.

It is interesting that even those male writers who address problems of welfare from a radical or Marxist perspective appear to remain rather blind to the way in which a nurturant role restricted to women has been enshrined within the welfare state.
(E. Wilson, Feminism and social policy', in M. Loney, D. Boswell and J. Clarke (eds), *Social Policy and Social Welfare*, Open University Press, 1983)

Pascall points out that even where Marxists have considered gender they have concentrated on the relationship between women and capitalism – the work that women do in the home supporting the reproduction of labour. They do not consider, she argues, the patriarchal relationship between men and women, yet the welfare state cannot be explained solely in terms of capitalism and the need for a healthy, cared-for labour force. That is, Marxists have treated reproduction as secondary to production in their analyses.

The Welfare State, then, may be seen as public control of the private sphere, and increasing male control of female work. Most obviously, the biology of reproduction has become the property of male medicine. But the family has also lost control of significant aspects of reproductive work to the male-dominated professions of medicine, teaching, and social work.
(G. Pascall, *Social Policy – a Feminist Analysis*, Tavistock, 1986)

The male-centred activities of the welfare state cannot be explained by an analysis which focuses on political economy. Rather, we need to consider why it is that most men do not see themselves in terms of people who could undertake the nurturing role in the family. After all, it is possible to argue that the needs of capitalism would be satisfied regardless of which people undertake waged work, and which people undertake unwaged work in the family, and there are many families where both partners undertake waged work and, also, where neither has a full-time job. However, we should also note that class and gender are not always exclusive. For example, it is often the case that middle-class women are responsible for acting as agents of the welfare state as social workers, teachers and so on, thereby performing the control functions that feminists have criticised.

Discrimination and the welfare state

In all of the principal areas of the welfare state – education, housing, health, income maintenance and the personal social services – there is evidence of discrimination against women in favour of men. Girls are treated differently from boys in the classroom; women find it more difficult than men to gain access to housing; patterns of health are gendered; and so on. However, the welfare state can also be seen to discriminate according to race and generation, and it is a major criticism of theories of the welfare state – not least the recent attempts at a critical social policy – that questions of race and of age have been relatively ignored.

Race and the welfare state

Catherine Jones argues in *Immigration and Social Policy in Britain* (Tavistock, 1977) that an examination of the treatment of migrants to Britain is a good test of the effectiveness of the welfare state. She examines the settlement of groups of migrants to Britain, from Irish settlement in the nineteenth century to post-war Afro-Caribbean and Asian settlement. She found that in each case there were similar responses from the native British. In different ways each group of immigrants was met in terms of posing a threat to law and order, a threat to health and an economic threat. In order to understand this typical reaction we need to consider the origins and nature of racism in Britain.

British racism can be identified before the sixteenth century and has continued to develop until it has become an inherent aspect of British culture. It is an ideology and practice which distinguishes between people solely on the basis of appearance, and can be found to be endemic in many institutions. This pervasive hostility to people of different ethnic backgrounds can be seen in the welfare state, where both direct and indirect racist practices occur. Black people in Britain are more likely than white people to be living in overcrowded or shared accommodation which lack amenities; they are more likely to live in older buildings and less likely to live in council accommodation or owner-occupied accommodation. Although discrimination is now outlawed, it is still possible to find evidence of welfare state agents using their discretionary power to discriminate against ethnic minorities (see Figure 5.2).

Figure 5.2 **Race and housing**
This extract illustrates how councils perceive race as a problem, and how they have the discretion to discriminate.

> In one area the council realised that on housing need grounds they would soon be rehousing a significant number of Asian families. Having settled in the area and only able to get the worst accommodation, these families would be at the top of the housing list as soon as the required five-year qualification was reached. The Labour-controlled council stopped all rehousing from the list and devised a new housing list scheme to give more weight to people with long local connections. The actual reasons behind the changes would probably never have been known if the chairman, in introducing them to the press had not blurted out 'if we had not taken this step we would have been rehousing nothing but Asians in five years'.
>
> (Community Development Project, *Limits of the Law*, CDP Inter-Project Editorial Team, 1977)

The Rampton Report of 1980 identified racism as one of the principle causes for the relative lack of achievement by West Indian children in British schools. This situation is exacerbated by the belief, held by some people, that immigrants entered this country with the intention of 'living off the welfare state'. In fact, this belies the truth that, first, an increasing proportion of black people were born in Britain and are not immigrants; it is a common mistake, one which constantly needs rectifying, to confuse immigration with race. Second, black people tend to use welfare services less than white people because, overall, the black populations in Britain are relatively younger than white populations,-and also black people often have a mistrust of the state, including the welfare state.

In 1976, for example, nearly two hundred Asian women attending antenatal clinics in Leicester were told to produce their passports. One woman who refused – and who had

previously had a confinement at the hospital – was denied treatment. Another case showed the links which can exist between
different parts of the state. A hospital clerk checked a patient's
immigration status with the Department of Health and Social
Security, who in turn checked with the Home Office. The
clerk received an answer within minutes.

    (Pal Luthra and Paul Gordan, 'Outlawing Immigrants, 2: the
    Bestways Passport Raid and Britain's Internal Immigration
    Controls', in Phil Scraton and Paul Gordon (eds), *Causes for
    Concern*, Penguin, 1984)

Third, black people were encouraged to migrate to Britain after
the Second World War to fill the job vacancies created by a labour
shortage – particularly in low paid and unpleasant jobs. Fourth,
rather than exploit the welfare state we may consider the contributions that black people make towards its development. One of
the biggest recruiters of labour after the war was the National
Health Service. **Lesley Doyal, Geoff Hunt and Jenny Mellor**
describe how the NHS is 'heavily reliant' on migrant doctors:
nearly a third of all NHS doctors come from abroad, mainly from
India. Similarly, in 1975, over a fifth of student and pupil nurses
had come from abroad, and, with some regional variations, a high
proportion of ancillary workers, mostly women (see Doyal, Hunt
and Mellor, 'Your life in their hands: migrant workers in the
NHS', *Critical Social Policy*, Feb. 1981; and, Lesley Doyal and
Imogen Pennell, *The Political Economy of Health*, Pluto Press,
1979).

    The British economy and the welfare state could be said to have
benefited from the immigration of people from different countries. However, as a consequence of discrimination many of these
people have considerable unmet needs, including a lack of recognition of quite particular needs such as the need for protection
(see Figure 5.3).

    As a result of the different cultural backgrounds additional
needs may develop – for example, in undertaking social work
with older black people (see Figure 5.4).

Age and generation

The demographic structure of Britain is changing; we are an
ageing society.

Figure 5.3 **Racial harassment**
The following case-study illustrates the need for protection
of many black families:

H FAMILY

This family is the only black household on their estate,
and has for years been the target for attack and
harassment.

Umpteen threats of violence, and indeed of 'death' have
been made, and Mr H dares not leave his family alone,
because of the constant vandalism and abuse. The car
which Mr H bought to travel to and from work was
extensively damaged and set on fire; within a few days
of its purchase, the replacement car was given the same
treatment. Both incidents were reported to the police,
but Mr H was advised that nothing could be done and
advised to take out a private summons. The District
Housing did not take Mr H's complaints seriously, and
the family continues to live in a state of terror and
dejection.

(The London Race and Housing Forum, *Racial Harassment on Local Authority Housing Estates*, Commission for
Racial Equality, 1981)

The number of people aged 65 or over is now over one and
a half times greater than in 1951, and in 1968 the number
represented just over 15 per cent of the population compared
with nearly 11 per cent in 1951. The number has grown by 3.2
million since 1951 and is expected to increase by another 2.6
million by the year 2025. The slow-down in projected growth
is due to the effects of low birth rates in the late 1920s and the
1930s. However, within the broad 65 or over age band, the
balance of different age groups is expected to change; those
aged 65 to 74 are projected to make up 53 per cent of those
aged 65 or over in 2025, compared with 57 per cent in 1986.
(Central Statistical Office, *Social Trends*, 18, HMSO, 1988)

A number of assumptions about the ageing process are taken
for granted which need to be considered before we examine the

Figure 5.4 **Old and black**
West Indian families have different expectations about care for older people than British families; this extract illustrates the concern that older West Indian people may not be cared for by their children.

All the respondents who had children who were brought up in the West Indies were confident that their children would fulfil their 'obligations' to them in the future and that they need have no fears of being rejected as they grew older. They did feel, however, that the next generation of elderly people would not be so fortunate as young blacks born in Britain were adopting different attitudes to the elderly; they did not 'appreciate' old people in the traditional way.

In my country always the young look after the old . . . grandma . . . she get very old . . . anyway, she still there because you don't put them away.

We usually don't keep our old people in an institution. We look after them. You don't leave them like how they done here, everybody live very close.

When your parents come old you just desert them and put them in a home for somebody else to take care of them. . . . Coloured people are different.

(Jo Cooper, 'West Indian elderly in Leicester', in Juliet Cheetham, Walter James, Martin Loney, Barbara Mayar and William Prescott (eds), *Social and Community Work in a Multi-Racial Society*, Harper & Row, 1981)

effectiveness of the welfare state in meeting the needs of older people. The picture that is often drawn is of a population that is enduring declining health and agility; is isolated and lonely, and is dependent on others for care and support. The evidence, however, leads us to question some of the assumptions that inform this view of ageing.

1 Decline in physical and mental health is not an inevitable part of getting older.

2 Although retirement from paid work has become virtually

universal (though not retirement from unpaid work for women), there is considerable evidence that many people do not wish to retire and do not enjoy retirement, particularly since it is likely to lead to a considerable reduction in income.

3 A majority of older people are capable of doing most things for themselves.

4 There are different age-groups within the taken-for-granted category of 'older person'; we may find, for example, a sixty-three-year-old woman looking after her eighty-five-year-old mother.

5 There is a real problem with incomes for older people, particularly since women live longer than men, yet are less protected in relation to occupational pension schemes.

Peter Townsend argues that older people are made to be dependent rather than dependency occurring as a function of some sort of natural decline. He argues that the capitalist organisation of work has created this *structured dependency*, creating an ideology of old age (see Figure 5.5). Once created, the dependency of older people becomes institutionalised. We may argue, therefore, that many of the substantial needs of older people are socially created rather than naturally produced. However, all the evidence shows that in terms of income, housing, health and personal social service, the welfare state has been very unsuccessful at meeting these needs. This leads to older people having to rely on their families, which in turn often means relying on their daughters or daughters-in-law, for care and support.

Young people

We must also recognise the dependency that the welfare state creates for younger people who may well experience it for the first time as something which controls and regulates their lives rather than gives them support. New legislation now requires unemployed young adults to enter training programmes, and changes to the board and lodgings regulations and social security entitlement mean that many young people are dependent on their families until the age of twenty-five. There is little, if any, housing provision for the young homeless in most areas, and if they do not have a family or relatives to support them they have

Figure 5.5 **Ageism**

At times both of high unemployment and relatively 'full' employment retirement has come to be used as one of the most important strategies for adjusting the numbers and structure of the labour force, with the additional advantage that it is much more acceptable to the unions than some other options. Perhaps for different reasons both management and unions have come to accept the expendability of older workers. The accelerated rate of technological change, and the successive adoption of new forms of training and educational qualifications, have contributed in no small measure to the over-valuation of the productive capacity of younger workers and the under-valuation of the productive capacities of older workers.

(Peter Townsend, 'Ageism and social policy', in Chris Phillipson and Alan Walker (eds), *Ageing and Social Policy*, Gower Publishing Co., 1986)

to depend on friends or enter the circuit of night shelters, hostels and 'crash-pads'.

Conclusion

By examining sociological theories of the welfare state we can advance our analysis beyond simply describing the changes in social policy that have taken place since its inception in 1948. Although there are competing aspects of sociological theory in the context of social welfare, most sociologists would agree that class, gender, race and age are most significant in understanding our relationship to the welfare state.

6 Conclusion – the future of the welfare state

The purpose of this chapter is to illustrate the contribution that sociologists can make to the study of social policy by examining the notion that there is a 'crisis' in the welfare state. This discussion demonstrates, once more, that we need to be wary of the uncritical expression of political values in any consideration of the future of the welfare state. Following the changes made in social policy since 1979 and the reductions in social provision it is difficult to sustain the notion that the welfare state is gradually evolving or improving. A sociological analysis of the future of the welfare state, therefore, might enable us to look beyond the political rhetoric which, from a left-wing point of view, suggests that welfare provision has been greatly reduced, and from a right-wing point of view suggests that provision by private as well as state organisations has resulted in a more efficient delivery of services.

Crisis in the welfare state

British governments in the 1970s responded to economic problems by reducing or curtailing welfare policies. Since 1979 Conservative governments have had a policy of reducing state welfare, looking to the private sector to replace public services. This has prompted a number of people to investigate the idea that there is a 'crisis in the welfare state'. In particular, commentators have developed the notion of *legitimation crisis* in attempting to identify the future of the welfare state.

Legitimation crisis and the welfare state

We may recall the Marxist argument that the welfare state in capitalist societies is an important agency in securing political consensus and maintaining social order. If the welfare state is unable to deliver services or is deliberately reduced in its scope, support for the welfare state and for government in general may be threatened. This is not inevitable and **Norman Johnson**, following one of the most influential writers on legitimation, Habermas, distinguishes between problems and crises:

> There is a crucially important distinction to be drawn between the existence of problems and a crisis. Problems will only lead to crisis if they cannot be contained or resolved and result in a loss of stability threatening the political and economic institutions of a society.
>
> (Norman Johnson, *The Welfare State in Transition*, Wheat-sheaf Books, 1987)

In answering the question of whether there is a crisis in the welfare state, **George** and **Wilding** suggest two ways in which the notion might be sustained; decline in support for the welfare state and an increase in social conflict. They demonstrate that there is evidence that the welfare state is less popular now than in the past, and there is also evidence of increased conflict such as the 'disturbances' in 1981 and 1985. However, George and Wilding do not think that these problems amount to a crisis; after all, there has never been a time when the welfare state could be said to have been successful in fully meeting its aims; the NHS has never had sufficient money to satisfy health needs; in the period of expansion in the 1960s there were still problems of homelessness; despite the rhetoric of equal opportunity the inequalities which existed in education in 1944 have largely persisted, and so on. Perhaps the difference in support for the welfare state is one of scale, rather than a complete lack of support.

The future of welfare

The welfare state may not have reached a crisis point threatening government legitimacy but it does seem to be changing in its nature and scope. The sociological examination of the welfare state enables us to consider these changes and identify possible future trends.

A sociological analysis can also identify strategies which have not been successful in the past; any future development must take account of unsuccessful attempts at improving the welfare state.

Incrementalism

A common response when a service has been unsuccessful in meeting its aims is to suggest an increase in spending – adding an incremental amount to the existing budget. Undoubtedly, most areas of welfare would benefit from more money. However, the reason for failure may include problems in the structure of service delivery. For example, there is a growing concern about the care of older people in private homes – problems of ill health, poor treatment and abuse from staff. Spending more money on the care of older people may help, but there is no guarantee that the abuse and neglect would end. It is useful to compare private homes in Britain where staff are in complete control and residents must 'do as they are told' with some of the homes in the USA or Eastern Europe where the residents are in charge of the establishment; they are responsible for appointing staff, for management, even for deciding the weekly menu.

Managerialism

A second solution that is often suggested is to attempt to improve the efficiency of a service by changing the management structure of an organisation. For example, the Seebohm Report, 1968, led to the creation of large social services departments in order to rationalise social work services and avoid duplication. Even with initial increased budgets these new departments have been unable to satisfy social service needs. With current decreases in budgets they have now reached a point where, in some areas, social work clients have to be put on waiting lists or they are simply not seen at all.

For George and Wilding the reason why these strategies have not worked lies in the social and economic structure within which the welfare state operates. Welfare is seen to be secondary to the principal values in capitalist societies of individualism, competition and achievement. They argue that unless these are replaced by values of co-operation and equality, which lead to a setting of needs above economic considerations, welfare will continue to be in a state of crisis.

Mishra, on the other hand, argues in *The Welfare State in Crisis* that neither the 'radical right' nor the 'radical left' offer positive and workable proposals for the future development of the welfare state. With regard to the former, Mishra argues that the *laissez-faire* values would lead to a situation where the 'weak would go to the wall'.

> A return to the free-market, to de-regulation, amounts to a counter-revolution. It means the dis-establishment of a variety of rights which do something towards maintaining minimum standards and providing a context within which the struggle against inequities can be waged.
>
> (R. Mishra; *The Welfare State in Crisis*, The Harvester Press, 1984)

Mishra finds a Marxist-socialist alternative to have fundamental drawbacks as well. By placing collectivistic and distributional aims as central to development, the rights and freedoms of the individual might be lost. Further, he argues that the problem of organising production without forcing people to work or providing material incentives has yet to be solved in socialist societies.

Instead, he commends a *corporatist welfare state* as a desirable alternative for the future. First, he reminds us that public support for welfare is still high and, second, economic recession requires the provision of some form of economic security, including the pursuit of full employment. To do this effectively requires the powerful groups in society to come together to agree economic and social policies. The leaders of these groups, usually taken to be trade unions, the state, and business organisations, become responsible for social and economic planning. This means that decisions are taken centrally by a relatively few elite people, and outside the parliamentary process.

Although there are different types of corporatism, a number of general criticisms can be made. As we have seen, decisions are taken centrally by an elite who are not elected and therefore not accountable to the society for which they take decisions. Corporatism relies on a political consensus for it to be sustained. However, it does not address questions of equality, and the inequalities in power between capital and labour. If one accepts that this relationship is one of opposing interests, sooner or later the legitimacy of corporatism will be challenged. For example, James Callaghan, who was a prime minister in the Labour government of 1974–79, attempted a corporatist solution to the problems facing the government with a 'social contract' between

Figure 6.1 **Decentralisation**

Decentralisation is seen by its proponents as valuable in reducing the power of the central state and as a prerequisite for successful participation, which is taken to mean involvement in both service delivery and policy-making. But the term 'decentralisation' in the welfare pluralist vocabulary does not simply mean a movement from central to local government. It also implies that local government, too, needs to be 'decentralised'. One means of achieving this secondary decentralisation is the patch system in which small teams of social workers serve neighbourhoods with about 10 000 inhabitants.

(Norman Johnson, *The Welfare State in Transition*, Wheatsheaf Books, 1987)

employers and trade unions. However, after only a short time industrial relations deteriorated, leading to a series of disputes which have come to be known as the 'Winter of Discontent' which in turn led to the downfall of the government.

Welfare pluralism

In contrast to the centralising tendency in corporatism, Johnson describes the recent trend towards *welfare pluralism* with its principal aims of *decentralisation* and *participation*. Decentralisation refers to the process of reducing state power in favour of a variety of organisations, especially at a local level. Participation is an accompanying process of encouraging a wider involvement in the decision-making processes (see Figure 6.1).

Johnson argues that welfare pluralism entails not only the state as a provider of welfare services but also an informal sector, a voluntary sector and a commercial sector. The informal sector refers to the work of the family, friends and neighbours in meeting needs. Indeed, it is these people who undertake the bulk of caring for others, usually unpaid, in Britain; and it is usually women in the family who actually do it. Although Conservative policies have celebrated this sector, they have been criticised, notably by feminists, for reinforcing the stereotype of the woman's role in the family at the same time as exploiting the work that women do in the home and for neighbours.

The voluntary sector has grown out of the nineteenth-century philanthropic tradition of 'helping the poor'. There are now a wide range of voluntary organisations, many of which have transcended the image of 'offering tea and sympathy' by having full-time paid organisers and extensive training requirements. They often satisfy needs that the other sectors have not addressed and may be organised around a single concern; marriage guidance, drug dependency (such as Alcoholics Anonymous), advice work (such as Citizens Advice Bureaux) and so on. Many of these, in turn, have become influential and respected pressure groups. Voluntary work has also been seen as one of the ways in which individuals can develop their altruistic concerns for others in the community and in the home.

The commercial sector refers to organisations which develop to satisfy needs in the context of private enterprise. Supporters of this sector see development of commercial services as a means of increasing competition and efficiency in service provision and extending freedom of choice. Critics, however, have argued that the existence of a commercial sector undermines the welfare state by allowing greater freedom of choice and more services only to those who can afford it, leaving a reduced service for everyone else. They argue that one cannot rely on a profit-making organisation to view the satisfaction of need as its prime concern.

Johnson demonstrates that welfare pluralism is currently favoured by the Conservative government, elected in 1987, although he does not see it as the most satisfactory organisation of welfare because it relies too heavily on the voluntary sector and the exploitation of women in the informal sector.

Separatism

J. Dale and P. Foster in *Feminists and State Welfare* (Routledge & Kegan Paul, 1986) address this exploitation and control of women in the welfare state. They examine the case for a separate welfare state for women as a solution to the continued control by men – as doctors, social services directors and so on. A separate service would be run by women for women. For example, they examine the women's health movement in the USA and the development of well-women clinics in Britain. Self-help is an important aspect of this 'separatist movement', such as the mutual support to be found in women's refuges.

Foster and Dale argue that separatist services for women exemplify a positive contribution to the development of welfare, particularly since they are often non-hierarchical and egalitarian organisations in contrast to the bureaucratic organisations usually found in the welfare state. However, separatist schemes often have difficulty in securing funding, and Foster and Dale also point out that many of the divisions of welfare which operate at the moment are rooted in capitalism as well as being patriarchal. What is required, they argue, is that the caring role should be given greater support in our society and it should not be considered the exclusive role of women.

Conclusion

A sociological examination of the notion of 'crisis in the welfare state' demonstrates that, despite the limitations on state welfare introduced since 1979 and the argument that this has provoked a crisis of legitimacy, welfare services are still being provided and the electorate have not yet lost complete faith in government.

We can see that the trend is towards welfare pluralism, so that many services which were provided by the state have been transferred to the other sectors. Critics, however, are not confident that welfare pluralism will advance the satisfaction of need any further than before 1979. Mishra looks to the examples of Sweden and Austria in his support for the development of a corporatist welfare state; feminists such as Dale and Foster have argued for a reappraisal of the caring role and for the provision of some separatist provision for women as well as adding their voices to the socialist claims of people such as George and Wilding, and Johnson, that the welfare state will only begin to succeed in fully meeting people's needs if it addresses the fundamental nature of inequality which is rooted in the realm of production in capitalist societies.

PART 3

Statistical data and documentary readings

---

7 Statistical data

Public expenditure in real terms

Table 7.1 shows the amount of public expenditure allocated by the government. The Conservative government led by Margaret Thatcher and committed to reducing public expenditure was in power throughout the period 1979–87.

Questions and activities (Table 7.1)

1 Identify which functions have had an increase in their budgets and which have had a decrease.
2 Discuss the possible reasons for these increases and decreases.
3 What effects, if any, have changes in public expenditure had on people's lives?

Statistical data on health services

Table 7.2a identifies the use of NHS hospitals according to speciality with fewer people staying in hospital, and for shorter periods. Table 7.2b demonstrates that expenditure on the NHS increased between 1980 and 1986, and shows how this expenditure was allocated within the NHS, with hospitals and community health services receiving the largest share.

Although expenditure on the NHS has increased, Table 7.2c shows that waiting lists for treatment have generally increased overall.

Table 7.1 Public expenditure in real terms[1]: by function

United Kingdom

Function	£s million (base year 1985–86)						
	1981–82	1982–83	1983–84	1984–85	1985–86	1986–87	1987–88
Function							
Defence	15 548	16 592	17 106	18 220	17 959	18 075	17 610
Overseas aid and other overseas services	1 951	2 409	2 793	2 948	2 688	2 988	2 752
Agriculture, fisheries, food and forestry	2 061	2 483	2 674	2 556	2 883	2 269	2 507
Industry, energy, trade and employment	9 121	7 580	7 473	9 403	6 969	6 756	5 786
Arts and libraries	803	840	852	881	876	942	921
Transport	6 288	6 058	5 838	5 878	5 559	5 726	5 807
Housing	5 206	4 380	4 827	4 646	3 939	3 854	4 157
Other environmental services	4 967	5 187	5 298	5 255	4 947	5 109	4 691
Law, order, and protective services	5 524	5 710	6 005	6 455	6 280	6 870	7 129
Education and Science	17 899	17 928	18 072	17 966	17 533	18 813	18 831
Health and personal social services	19 610	19 900	20 239	20 792	20 700	21 702	22 256
Social security	36 475	38 634	40 088	41 668	42 797	44 606	44 478
Other expenditure[2]	3 951	3 919	2 990	3 153	3 194	3 426	7 094
Privatisation proceeds	–611	–564	–1 262	–2 260	–2 702	–4 619	–4 687
Total public expenditure	128 793	131 057	132 994	137 563	133 622	136 500	139 331
Of which expenditure by:							
Local authorities[3]	32 920	33 638	36 657	37 027	35 231	37 600	37 664
Nationalised industries	4 401	2 476	2 526	4 057	1 709	959	649
Other public corporations	1 713	1 496	997	1 155	931	820	933

1 Real terms figures are cash outturns or plans adjusted to 1985–86 price levels by excluding the effect of general inflation as measured by the GDP deflator.

2 Includes miscellaneous expenditure, local authority current expenditure not allocated to function, the Reserve, and, in 1986–87, allowances for the difference between the assessment of the likely outturn expenditure and the sum of the other items shown and the external finance for nationalised industries which were privatised.

3 Excludes finance for nationalised industries and other public corporations.

Source: The Government's Expenditure Plans (CM 50), HM Treasury; cited in Central Statistical Office, *Social Trends*, 18, 1988.

Table 7.2a NHS hospital summary

	1971	1976	1981	1982	1983	1984	1985
All in-patients							
Discharges and deaths (thousands)	6 437	6 525	7 179	6 854[4]	7 461	7 666	7 884
Average number of beds available daily[1] (thousands)	526	484	450	428[4]	440	429	421
Average number of beds occupied daily (thousands)							
Maternities	19	16	15	14[4]	14	14	13
Other patients	417	378	350	331[4]	340	333	327
Total – average number of beds occupied daily	436	394	366	345[4]	354	347	341
Average length of stay (days)							
Medical patients	14.7[4]	12.1	10.2[4]	9.9[4]	9.5	9.1	8.7
Surgical patients	9.1[4]	8.6	7.6[4]	7.6[4]	7.2	6.9	6.7
Maternities	7.0[4]	6.7	5.6[4]	5.3[4]	5.1	4.9	4.7
Private in-patients[2] (thousands)							
Discharges and deaths	115	95	98	82	84	79	—
Average number of beds occupied daily	2	2	1	1	1	1	—
New out-patients[3] (thousands)							
Accidents and emergency	9 358	10 463	11 342	11 225[4]	11 932	12 279	12 492
Other out-patients	9 572	9 170	9 816	9 577[4]	10 119	10 376	10 604
Average attendances per new patient (numbers)							
Accidents and emergency	1.6	1.6	1.4	1.4[4]	1.4	1.4	1.3
Other out-patients	4.2	4.0	4.4	4.4[4]	4.3	4.3	4.3
Day case attendances (thousands)	—	565[4]	863	844[4]	979	1 081	1 166

1 Staffed beds only
2 England and Wales only
3 The 1971 and 1976 figures for out-patients in Scotland include ancillary departments.
4 Great Britain only
Source: Department of Health and Social Security; Scottish Health Service, Common Services Agency; Welsh Office; Department of Health and Social Services, Northern Ireland

Table 7.2b Public expenditure on the NHS, Great Britain (£ million)

	1980–81	1984–85[1]	1985–86[1]
Current expenditure			
Hospitals and community health services	8 339	11 056	11 725
Family practitioner services	2 561	4 019	4 277
Central health and miscellaneous services	347	554	594
Capital expenditure			
Hospitals and community health services	631	908	910
Family practitioner services	5	7	10
Central health and miscellaneous services	14	46	44
Total	11 897	16 590	17 560

1 From April 1983 Departments repay PSA for accommodation and certain other services under the new Repayment Service.
Source: HM Treasury

Table 7.2c Hospital in-patient waiting lists[1], United Kingdom (thousands)

	1976	1981	1983	1984	1985
Specialty					
General surgery[2]	200.5	169.1	197.4	183.3	174.0
Orthopaedics	109.8	145.1	170.9	165.4	154.1
Ear, nose, or throat	121.7	115.4	134.1	128.8	128.7
Gynaecology	91.8	105.6	114.4	107.4	107.1
Oral surgery	26.5	35.5	51.8	55.3	55.1
Plastic surgery	44.7	49.2	51.3	50.4	46.0
Ophthalmology	41.2	43.4	51.4	53.4	55.2
Urology[3]	22.0	29.1	38.5	39.2	38.9
Other	42.5	44.2	44.7	44.6	43.4
All specialties	700.8	736.6	854.5	827.9	802.6

1 Waiting lists of NHS hospitals only as at 30 September each year, except for the Northern Ireland figures for 1982 which are as at 31 March.
2 Includes the Northern Ireland figures for 'Urology'.
3 Great Britain only
Source: Department of Health and Social Security; Scottish Health Service, Common Services Agency; Welsh Office; Department of Health and Social Services, Northern Ireland
(Tables 7.2a–c were cited in *Social Trends*, 17, 1987.)

Questions and activities (Table 7.2)

1 Using Tables 7.2a–c, identify trends in hospital work.
2 What reasons might there be for the fluctuations in the numbers of people waiting for treatment?
3 Discuss the apparent contradiction that more money has been spent on the NHS, yet waiting lists have generally got longer and fewer people are staying in hospital.

Attitudes to welfare

The continued election, in the 1980s, of Conservative governments pledged to reduce public provision might suggest that popular support for the welfare state has declined. Tables 7.3a–c illustrate what attitudes the public have towards welfare.

In 1984 people were asked what their priorities would be for extra public spending:

Table 7.3a Priorities for extra public expenditure

	First priority (%)	Second priority (%)
Health	51	25
Education	20	29
Help for industry	10	10
Housing	6	12
Social security	7	8
Police and prisons	1	5
Defence	3	3
Roads	1	3
Overseas aid	★	1
Public transport	★	1

Note: Owing to the effects of rounding data the figures do not always total 100%.
A ★ denotes a percentage of less than 0.5.
Source: R. Jowell and S. Witherspoon (eds), *British Social Attitudes – the 1985 Report*, Gower, 1985

Table 7.3b The welfare state makes people nowadays less willing to look after themselves:

	1983 (%)	1985 (%)
Agree strongly/just agree	52	44
Neither agree nor disagree	21	23
Just disagree/disagree strongly	26	32

Source: R. Jowell, S. Witherspoon and L. Brook (eds), *British Social Attitudes – the 1986 Report*, Gower, 1986

Table 7.3c Suppose the government had to choose between the three options (below), which do you think it should choose?

	1983 (%)	1984 (%)	1985 (%)
Reduce taxes and spend *less* on health, education and social benefits	9	6	6
Keep taxes and spending on these services *at the same level as* now	54	50	43
Increase taxes and spend *more* on health, education and social benefits	32	39	45

Source: R. Jowell, S. Witherspoon and L. Brook (eds), *British Social Attitudes – the 1986 Report*, Gower, 1986

Questions and activities (Table 7.3)

1 What do Tables 7.3a–c reveal about the nature of support for social welfare?
2 What additional evidence would be useful to assess the claim that the welfare state does or does not have popular support?
3 Using the same questions, undertake a similar survey of attitudes amongst your peers, parents and others. Afterwards, attempt an explanation of why they hold a particular set of attitudes.

Housing

Table 7.4 illustrates the changes in the number of houses available between 1961 and 1985 and also who was responsible for those changes.

Table 7.4 Changes in dwelling stock, United Kingdom (thousands)

	1961–1970	1971–1975	1976–1980	1981	1982	1983	1984	1985
New construction								
Local authorities	152	118	105	58	36	37	35	29
New town corporations	9	12	12	10	4	2	2	1
Housing associations	4	10	21	19	13	16	17	13
Government departments	5	2	1	1	—	—	—	—
Total public sector	170	143	139	88	54	55	54	43
Private sector	198	178	146	118	127	148	158	154
Total new construction	368	320	284	206	180	203	212	197
Other changes								
Slum clearance	−65	−64	−45	−37	−26	−20	−15	−12
Other[1]	−44	−34	−4	−13	+7	+3	+1	+7
Total other changes	−109	−98	−49	−50	−19	−17	−14	−5
Total net gain	258	222	235	156	161	186	198	192

[1] Comprises net gains from conversions and other causes, and losses other than by slum clearance.
Source: Department of the Environment; cited in Social Trends, 17, 1987

Table 7.5 Income distribution by households, United Kingdom (percentages and £s per week)[1]

	Percentage of all households	Percentage of reported expenditure									Average total expenditure £s per week (= 100%)
		Food	Housing	Fuel and light	Alcohol	Tobacco	Clothing and footwear	Durable household goods	Transport and vehicles	Other goods, services, miscellaneous	
Pensioner households[2]											
Low income	14	26.0	20.8	13.2	2.5	2.8	5.3	3.9	5.3	20.4	55.79
Other	12	20.6	21.6	7.9	3.4	2.1	5.4	6.1	12.0	20.8	122.66
One-parent households											
Low income	1	30.9	7.2	13.8	2.5	6.5	10.7	5.6	5.2	17.6	62.25
Other	2	23.8	14.6	8.2	2.1	3.3	10.8	5.0	11.1	21.2	111.42
Other households with children											
Low and middle income	22	23.7	14.8	6.6	4.2	3.4	8.1	7.1	13.9	18.2	164.84
High income	8	18.3	14.8	4.6	4.8	1.7	8.7	8.8	15.0	23.2	307.83
One person households[3]											
Low income	3	23.5	18.4	11.2	4.8	5.1	5.5	3.3	11.2	17.0	57.24
Other	7	14.8	20.1	5.0	5.9	2.4	6.0	6.7	19.1	20.1	128.76
Other households without children											
Low income	1	23.7	17.0	9.7	5.0	5.0	5.2	4.3	15.8	14.2	100.71
Middle income	19	20.1	15.9	6.0	5.7	3.4	6.8	7.8	15.9	18.4	165.78
High income	11	16.9	14.0	4.1	6.2	2.1	7.7	7.3	19.5	22.2	294.40
All households	100	20.2	16.1	6.1	4.9	2.7	7.4	7.2	15.2	20.2	161.87
Low income	20	25.7	18.8	12.4	3.2	3.7	5.8	4.0	7.7	18.8	60.70
Middle income	60	21.3	16.7	6.5	4.7	3.1	7.2	7.1	14.6	18.8	150.62
High income	20	17.4	14.5	4.4	5.6	1.5	8.0	8.0	17.6	22.7	296.81

1 The income distribution used is that of disposable household income – low income is defined here as the lowest 20 per cent of this income distribution, middle income as the next 60 per cent and high income the highest 20 per cent.
2 Pensioner households are defined as those households solely containing one or two persons of pensionable age.
3 Excludes pensioners.
Source: Central Statistical Office, from Family Expenditure Survey; cited in *Social Trends*, 18, 1988

Questions and activities (Table 7.4)

1 What are the trends in housing construction? How would you explain these trends?
2 What implications do these trends have for any future housing policy and the satisfaction of housing need?
3 Find out what developments in housing stock are taking place in the area where you live; e.g., is there a slum clearance programme; a programme of new construction and so on?

Household expenditure

Table 7.5 illustrates the different proportions of their incomes that households spend on various categories of consumption.

Questions and activities (Table 7.5)

1 What differences are there in the consumption patterns of the different social groups; how would you explain these differences?
2 What does the table reveal about the existence of needs?
3 What items of household expenditure do you think are included in 'Other goods, services, miscellaneous'?
4 Attempt to calculate what you consider to be the minimum budget for your household.

8 Readings and activities

Reading 1

Sociological ideas are often to be found in fiction. Zoe Fairburns' futuristic novel *Benefits* describes what life might be like for poor people in the not too distant future.

> Ninety-six flats had meant more than twice that many children; but once the older boys had staked territorial claims to the grass patch, no one young or weak got a look in. The boys found other sources of fun: filling the lift with bricks, tying door knockers together, calling in the fire-brigade. Windows got smashed. Families withheld rent and were evicted; or vanished overnight, leaving massive arrears and furniture that had not been paid for. Childish spirits turned malignant. Paraffin was poured through letterboxes and lit; human shit was left on landings; bricks and planks and crockery were thrown from high windows. Soon anyone with any choice in the matter moved out of the flats, leaving behind only those with no choice. Teenage mothers who looked forty. Drunken, shuffling, unemployed men. Ragged litters of children, yelling as they slithered down the endless banisters or hung from high windows to terrorise passers-by. Old folk with multiple locks on the doors, peering out at the stray dogs that met and fought and mated in the corridors.
>
> (Zoe Fairburns, *Benefits*, Virago, 1979)

Questions ad activities

1 In what ways does a fictional account of social life differ from that of the sociologist?

2 Do you think that this account of the future is accurate? Give reasons for your answer.

3 How would a sociologist explain the older boys' behaviour?

Reading 2   *Community care and older people*

Community care has become a popular solution to the problem of how to look after those people who are unable to look after themselves; popular, that is, for the people who have the task of finding solutions such as politicians, social services managers and so on. The people being looked after often have a different story to tell, as this article based on a television documentary, *The Granny Business*, demonstrates.

'A LICENCE TO PROFIT FROM ABUSE OF THE ELDERLY'

The government's policy of 'community care' for the elderly has provided the owners of private homes with a huge potential clientele. Hospitals are cutting the number of beds in their geriatric wards, discouraging longstay patients, and getting the elderly back into the 'community' as soon as possible. . . .

But council provision for support services falls well below the standards stipulated by the DHSS. For example, no less than 80 per cent of local authorities fail to provide the required number of home helps for the aged. There were actually fewer meals and home helps being provided for people over 75 per thousand of the population in the early eighties than there had been in the mid-seventies. As councils cut back on their own residential homes, the elderly have had no alternative but to turn to the mushrooming private sector. It is often the hospitals and the local councils who place them there.

The result has been an unprecedented boom in private residential homes for the elderly throughout Britain. The number of old people in such homes has trebled since 1974. If, as is often the case, they have assets of less than £3000, the DHSS foots the bill. . . .

The reality of private care for the elderly can be very different from the government ideal. There are, of course, exceptions. But many of those being paid to care for elderly people are simply ill-equipped to do so with the expertise and compassion which such specialised and demanding work requires. The average level of care is limited and unimaginative. Without stimulation, residents age and stagnate. The typical scene in such homes is of a sparsely furnished lounge fringed with institutional armchairs in which residents pass the day in unattended torpor, unenlivened by the television blaring relentlessly from one corner.

In fact, it seems the more they need care, the less likely old people are to get any. Distressed staff who had worked at the Anglia, a home in Canterbury, told of how one old lady regularly saw no one all day and was frequently to be found in urine-soaked clothes, sometimes face-down in her food. . . .

The irony is that places like the Anglia are seen as sanctuaries by those elderly people who have had to live in homes where there is active abuse. Take, for instance, the Pottertons' home for the elderly in Faversham – on the face of it, clean and well run. But few visitors to the home ever saw how the most frail and confused residents were treated in the upstairs rooms where they spent most of their days. Former staff report that incontinent old ladies at the Pottertons' had no heating at night and wore pyjama tops only. They lay on polythene, covered in a thin tatty sheet. Their blankets were filthy with excrement. They were woken at 5.30 a.m. and the urine-drenched poly-thene had to be peeled off. They were often shouted at by Mrs Potterton, a trained nurse. On her instructions, they spent hours each day tied to commodes with an assortment of stock-ings and belts. One of them was beaten and bruised on her wrist with a slipper by Mrs Potterton, apparently because she had wet herself . . . .

The home about which we received most complaints is in the heart of Thanet, just a few blocks away from the Margate beach. Staff who had worked at the home. . . gave us a detailed catalogue of incidents of cruel ill-treatment. . . .

Gangrenous sores were treated with talcum powder which care assistants were expected to put on with their bare hands. Residents were often tied up or deprived of food as a punish-ment for being 'difficult'. People who could not walk properly were taunted and forced to crawl up the home's long flight of stairs, sometimes screaming in pain. Mrs Newington [who ran the home] hit several residents, in one case punching an old woman named Annie full in the face because she was resisting sedation that was being administered by force. Staff described to us how drugs were systematically administered, often by force – totally counter to all current practice – and that Mrs Newington forced pills or liquid into residents' mouths and they fell to the floor in agony.

One care assistant summarised existence at the home: 'When people go there, they don't go there to retire or to relax, they don't go there to live, they go there to die.' Meanwhile, we estimate Mrs Newington's income from the home to be nearly £250 000.

(Mark Halliley, 'A licence to profit from abuse of the elderly', the *Listener*, 8 Oct. 1987)

Questions and activities

1 Why has there been a rapid growth in private residential homes for older people?
2 Why are older people abused, both in private residential homes and in the homes of their children where they also might be living? What differences are there between residential homes and family homes?
3 Find out all the places in your local areas where old people might live such as private residential homes, sheltered accommodation, private nursing homes, homes run by the social services, and so on. What sort of accommodation do you think is the most satisfactory for older people?

Reading 3   Rural poverty

In recent years social problems, especially poverty, have been most often related to the decline of the 'inner city'. However, as Brian McLaughlin's article shows, poverty is also to be found in the countryside – in contrast to the idyll that many people hold of living in a country village. (The article is based on research sponsored by the Department of the Environment and the Development Commission.)

Recent evidence from an investigation into deprivation in rural areas . . . indicates that in the 1980s many of our rural population are no strangers to poverty. Moreover, the fact that the rural poor exist amidst considerable affluence increases their relative deprivation to the point where it could be argued that, in many respects, the rural poor are worse off than their urban counterparts. . . .

The high incidence of poverty amongst elderly households in the rural areas reflects the high percentage of those households who were living on state pensions only, with a correspondingly low level of take-up of other entitlements. Rural pensioners are also disadvantaged by the inadequacy of occupational pensions based on the low wages of many rural occupations. In the case of other households, however, the primary cause of their poverty is low wages in the rural labour market. . . .

The full significance of the distribution of poverty in rural areas only becomes apparent when set in the broader context of rural policy. For example, a higher proportion of households in or on the margins of poverty lived in housing which lacked basic amenities such as an inside WC and a fixed bath or shower. That group was also most dependent upon public rented housing and, as such, most vulnerable to policies which reduce the stock of such housing in the rural context. The only real alternative for many was private rented tenures, but the availability of such housing in rural areas in the 1980s is often more apparent than real.

Within those rural areas covered by the survey, 40% of the private rented stock was job tied. For the remainder, keen competition existed between the low paid employees and higher income groups such as professional employees in the public and private sectors who were not earning enough to enter owner-occupation. As the latter could afford higher rents, the lower paid invariably lost out.

Households in or on the margins of poverty also recorded the lowest levels of personal mobility which, in the rural context, represents another critical dimension of poverty. Consequently, they depended on locally based and/or mobile facilities for many of their basic services . . . .

For those households without a car, the journey for medical treatment was often a greater ordeal than the illness for which treatment was being sought. For households with one car, the journey for treatment often meant the car-driver had to take time off work to act as a chauffeur, usually at a cost of lost time and money.

(Brian McLaughlin, 'Rural rides', *Poverty*, no. 63, Spring 1986)

Questions and activities

1 What do you think is meant by 'the fact that the rural poor live
  exist amidst considerable affluence increases their relative
  deprivation'?
2 What problems with housing do people on low incomes have
  in rural communities? What effects might tourism have on rural
  housing?
3 Compare the availibility of services such as access to shops,
  doctors and post offices in rural communities and urban
  communities. If you live close to a rural community try to
  find out what services actually exist. What problems would you
  have to resolve in order to research rural poverty?

Reading 4   Race and mental health

In this extract, Boyd Tonkin examines black people's experiences
of mental health policies.

> While their parents might have suffered in silence, the second
> generation of black Britons often encounters psychiatry at its
> most heavy-handed. . . .
>
> Yet young black men still account for an unusually high,
> proportion of compulsory assessments and treatments under
> sections 2 and 3 of the Mental Health Act, and of remands
> from courts to hospitals and secure units (sections 25–38).
>
> Irrefutable proof is hard to come by here, since until this year
> the Mental Health Act Commission (which oversees the treat-
> ment of patients detained under the Act) has not kept records
> of ethnic origins.
>
> But small-scale research has confirmed the impressions of
> many observers. Forensic psychiatrist Rosemary Cope found
> a larger number of Afro-Caribbean people in the West
> Midlands regional secure units than their distribution in the
> general population warranted.
>
> 'They're far more likely to be admitted as compulsory
> patients, often after the involvement of the police,' she
> reports. . . .
>
> For some years, black community groups have targeted
> complaints at section 136 of the Act, sometimes called a
> 'mental health sus law'. It gives police the power to detain a
> person in a public place who appears to be suffering from a

mental disorder, and to present a danger to himself or others. The person can then be removed and held for 72 hours at a 'place of safety'; usually a mental hospital in London, a police station or elsewhere.

Ann Rogers, a research officer with MIND, has discovered that among referrals to three London places of safety, Afro-Caribbeans did account for 31% of detentions under section 136, but only 10% of the local population. However, she believes that: 'The biggest factor in section 136 is social disadvantage, not ethnicity.'

. . . For Errol Francis of the Afro-Caribbean Mental Health Association, the psychiatric punishment of black people, from special schools to Rampton, merely reflects the bankruptcy of an entire discipline. 'Psychiatry is one of the worst ways of dealing with mental distress. If you're black, it comes through the prism of race; if you're female, through the prism of gender. But it's always the medical model that actually harms people.'

. . . Some professionals combine a critique of conventional psychiatry with an awareness of the depth of genuine disturbance among their black clients. They may trace episodes of distress and depression back to the racism that lowers the self-esteem and weakens the resistance of its victims.

(Boyd Tonkin, 'Black and blue', *Community Care*, 14 May 1987)

Questions and activities

1 Implicit in this extract are four explanations for the higher proportion of black people than white people being perceived as 'mentally ill'. What are they and which one, if any, do you think is the most valid?

2 What do you think Errol Francis means by 'But it's always the medical model that actually harms people'?

3 Why do we need to know about race and gender before we can understand the relationship between black people and mental health and women mental health?

Reading 5   The cost of child-rearing

Clearly, there is no single answer to the question: 'How much do children cost?' The answer varies according to the method used to estimate this cost and also according to the kind of living standard that is taken as the basis of the estimate. The answer also varies very considerably according to whether only direct (ie. money) costs of the needs of children are included or whether some estimate is also made of the lost opportunities for earning during the years of child-care or the value of the services that parents provide for children without payment.

Considering the indirect costs first, available estimates are tentative and few in number. These kinds of costs clearly require a great deal of further research. The best that can be said at the moment is that costs appear to be considerable: loss of earnings of the order of £130 per week or, alternatively, child-care services worth up to £200 per week.

In relation to direct costs of children, much more research has been done, but the results are not entirely consistent, always subject to methodological difficulties, and sometimes surrounded by controversy. By revaluing the result of norma-tive estimates of the minimum requirements of children to current (September 1986) price levels, it is possible, with some trepidation, to suggest that the cost of a child under ten, at the minimum standard consistent with any concept of humanity, is in the range £10 to £11 per week, and that the equivalent for a child aged eleven to fifteen is in the range £13.50 to £15.50 per week. With similar trepidation, the direct costs of children at a standard of living somewhat beyond this minimum, and consistent with some concept of normality, are within the ranges £17.50 to £21 for up to ten years olds and £27.50 to £33 for children over ten. It must be emphasised that these estimates are crude averages for these age groups as a whole. In the case of babies, it is clear that there are very substantial direct costs of special clothing and equipment which may amount to £700–£800.

(Deborah Mitchell and Kenneth Cooke, 'The costs of chil-drearing', in Robert Walker and Gillian Parker (eds), *Money Matters: Income, Wealth and Financial Welfare*, Sage Publica-tions, 1988)

Questions and activities

1 What is meant by 'direct' and 'indirect' costs of child-rearing?

2 Distinguish between the authors' use of 'normative' and 'normality' in relation to child-rearing.
3 The authors suggest that there are 'methodological problems' in researching the costs of child-rearing. How would you find out how much it costs to keep you or any other children?
4 Write down all the ways in which the state supports or subsidises the cost of rearing children.

Reading 6   Housing structure and design

The weak position of women in the labour market, and their responsibilities within the home as domestic workers and childrearers, affect not only women's access to housing, but its structure and design.

WORKING CONDITIONS IN THE HOME
Because the home is a workplace for women, they tend to spend more time there than men or children. Clearly, there are vast differences in this respect between married and unmarried women, mothers and non-mothers and those who do paid work as well as housework. However, it is generally the case that women do more housework than men. We would therefore argue that housing conditions are more important to them and their needs broader. Yet the home is regarded as a private sanctuary and conditions in the home are largely outside the law. Housewives are isolated, without the protection of their rights corresponding to those won by waged workers through trade union organisation and solidarity. There is no counterpart to the health and safety legislation of waged employment. Preschool child care, for example, when socialised and undertaken by registered childminders or in nurseries and creches, is subject to stringent regulations. It is hardly surprising that the highest number of accidents occur in the home.

DESIGN
Despite this relationship of women to the home, they have little control over the nature of their housing. Architects and planners are usually men and, in the case of local authority housing estates, not of the class of those who actually spend most of their time in the flats and houses they design. It is women who bear the brunt of high-rise flats, estates with no

open play spaces, inadequate laundry facilities, noise, vandalism and bad access to shops and transport. Cramped kitchens, damp, thin walls, broken lifts, dark and dangerous stairways and the numerous other consequences of low cost building, make taking care of the home and rearing young children doubly difficult and time consuming.

(Helen Austerberry and Sophie Watson, 'A woman's place: a feminist approach to housing in Britain', *Feminist Review*, no. 8, Summer 1981)

Questions and activities

1 Write down, in your own words, what you think the authors mean by 'The weak position of women in the labour market, and their responsibilities within the home as domestic workers and child-rearers, affect not only women's access to housing, but its structure and design'?
2 Why do you think men and women, typically, have different ideas about designing houses and planning communities?
3 Draw a plan of a typical house; now draw a plan of a house which would satisfy the needs that women have identified in housing; for example, what design would make it easier to do housework or look after children?
4 In a similar way, draw a street map of an area you are familar with; now prepare a street map which satisfies the needs identified in the extract; for example, making a community safer or making it easier to care for children. (You might find it useful to start with circles rather than squares; similarly, you might find it useful to consider the design of houses and villages in non-industrial societies.)

Reading 7   Altruism

Care can be seen as both natural and contrived, as at once needed and imposed, as simultaneously enhancing and impoverishing the lives both of those who received and of those who give. When we introduce the additional element of the neighbourhood the problem becomes even worse. Richard Titmuss attempted a distinction between gifts as tools and gifts as gifts, recognising the potentially coercive nature of giving and, most oddly, insisting on the importance of anonymity and

distance in social care as a means of eliminating the self-
oriented side-effects of altruism (people should be free to give
but not decide to whom they give; the recipients of care should
be 'strangers').

One strain of radical criticism of altruism holds that it is
intellectually fraudulent and socially pernicious. Historians
have repeatedly demonstrated the ways in which progressives
and reformers of all kinds have expected childishness from the
'dependent' as the price of care; the violation or surrender of
rights being justified through the unexamined application of
the equation: need = dependency = non-competence. Sociologists of caring institutions and agencies have identified
category upon category of caring agents as little more than a
sort of moral secret police. A great deal of care can be seen as
a 'coerced waiver of rights' on the back of economic inequity,
as an alternative to recognising the latter as the real
problem. . . .

Those of us who believe in neighbourhood care are stuck
with the task of defending an enterprise which devotees of
simple moralities will assail from all sides. We can do so in my
view only by asserting strenuously the pragmatic *desirability* of
contradiction, the morality of trying to have your cake and eat
it – that is, of working at both care *and* autonomy, both
Gemeinschaft and Gesellschaft. We can degrade people by caring
for them; and we can degrade them by not caring for them.
(Martin Bulmer, *Neighbours: the Work of Philip Abrams*,
Cambridge University Press, 1986)

Questions and activities

1 What does the author mean by describing care as being
'coercive'?
2 Why did Titmuss insist that altruism should be anonymous?
3 Prepare a list of five occasions where care is given; for example,
having a social worker or receiving advice about social
security entitlement. For each of these occasions, write down
what help is given and then write down what you consider
to be the 'coercive element' which induces dependency or
childishness.
4 What do you think the author is trying to suggest in the final
paragraph?

Reading 8   Sociology and social policy

Policy analysis must . . . depend on a broad sociological perspective about both objectives and means. Social policy is best conceived as a kind of blueprint for the management of society towards social ends: it can be defined as *the underlying as well as professed rationale by which social institutions and groups are used or brought into being to ensure social preservation or development.* Social policy is, in other words, the institutionalised control of services, agencies and organisations to maintain or change social structure and values. Sometimes this control may be utterly conscious, and consciously expressed by Government spokesmen and others. Sometimes it may be unspoken and even unrecognised.

In this sense of the term, then, all societies have social polices. In identifying the different policies of developing and advanced societies the sociologist may gradually call attention to the fact that policy analysis is independent of planning. The difference is essentially one between a· subjective orientation, even when that is expressed collectively by a community, a city or a nation, and one that strives to be objective. Policy analysis is the task of unravelling and evaluating the policy of a society, or, more correctly, the policies of different social groups and agencies, with government and industry being the predominant agencies in advanced industrial societies. Planning, by contradistinction, is best conceived as the search for alternative policies. It is the definition of goals on the basis of measured needs among (and between) populations and the development of a rational strategy and of appropriate means to fulfil those objectives most quickly.

(Peter Townsend, 'Sociology and social policy', in *Sociology and Social Policy*, Penguin Books, 1975)

Questions and activities

1 How does the author define social policy? What limitations are there with this definition?
2 What is the distinction between policy analysis and planning?
3 What is the relationship between sociology and social policy?

Readings 9 and 10   'Scroungerphobia'

Sociologists have argued that systems of poverty relief serve to control the poor and shame claimants in order to sustain a particular set of values. One of the ways in which claimants are currently 'blamed for their poverty' is through the mass media.

In the last six months of 1976, we analysed all the welfare and social security news, in the national press, and in the local press and radio in two cities. No fewer than 30.8 per cent of all stories dealt in some way with social security abuse, and in 12.6 per cent with legal proceedings. In other words, one in eight of all stories in all media in this period which were about social services, welfare or social security, dealt with criminal proceedings consequent on social security abuse.

This 'scroungerphobia' however, was merely the face of a more permanent hostility to public social and income support services, which is fixed deep in our culture and exhumed by periods of stress for the economic order.

'KIND HEARTS AND CON TRICKS'
The headline is from the *Daily Mirror* of 21 September 1976. Subtly, social security is transformed from an agency for the preservation of living standards into a policing mechanism for controlling scroungers and spongers. Social security clerks are portrayed as the naive victims of a guileful army of tricksters and swindlers, shelling out what a *Daily Mirror* headline called 'The Bonanza Paid in Error' (30 September 1977). The claimant becomes criminal – to be policed, checked, investigated, suspected and controlled.

Britain, it appears, is unusually lax in these matters. A *Sun* report (17 March 1978) tells us, 'It's not so easy to cadge from our Euro-pals.' Back home, 'We're more big-hearted with the taxpayers' money – or barmy, depending on how you look at it.'

The good life provided by welfare benefits is a target whenever benefits are uprated, an annual event since 1971. In 1976 it was 'Pay Code Breached by Welfare Rises' in the *Sunday Express*, and some curious arithmetic in several papers producing the mythical £5 000 a year dole-queue plutocracy. It became commonplace to repeat the refrain raised by Tory

MP Ralph Howell that 'it pays a man not to work'. In the *Daily Mail* it was 'How the £75 a week man is better off on the dole', while the *Daily Express* claimed confidently that 'millions of men might find it financially more worthwhile to be on the dole than at work' (15 November 1976). Since the dole for a single man had just risen to £12.90 the arithmetic was a little puzzling.

(Peter Golding and Sue Middleton, 'Why is the press so obsessed with welfare scroungers?', *New Society*, 26 Oct. 1978)

Following the rise in unemployment and government attempts to reduce public spending in the 1980s it might be argued that these harsh attitudes to claimants would have softened.

Many polls since the mid-1970s have demonstrated increasing support for spending on social services and welfare, even if it means no tax cuts or even increased taxation. Probed a little further these attitudes show a pattern. The health service continues to hold the affection of the majority. Research carried out three or four years ago, however, found that while people were harbouring substantial second thoughts about public expenditure cuts, their priority for renewed expenditure was law and order, or among social services, education. Welfare services, let alone benefits, seldom gained popular ranking . . . . research continues to show the vitality of scroungerphobia. Even in the *Breadline Britain* survey, one in five disagreed with the statement that 'most people claiming supplementary benefit are in real need'. A MORI poll carried out after the social security green paper was published last year, asked people to suggest what proportion of claimants they thought were fiddling, and obtained a median response of 28 per cent.

Attitudes are selective, discriminating, and continue to feed off the deep-rooted value placed on the principles of less eligibility and the undeserving poor. By and large, people support the services which support the rich – large spending areas like health and education whose political and economic arithmetic always turns out to show such surprising advantages for the better off.

(Peter Golding, 'Rich man, poor man', *New Society*, 18 April 1986)

Questions and activities

1 Why do the mass media portray claimants as 'scroungers' and 'fiddlers'?
2 In addition to newspaper stories, how else do the mass media present a derogatory image of claimants? (for example, in humour.)
3 For a period of time, such as a week or a month, examine a national newspaper, a local newspaper, television programmes and television news:
   (a) How much time is spent covering welfare issues?
   (b) How are claimants and recipients portrayed?
   (c) What differences are there, if any, between newspapers and television, between local and national newspapers, and between tabloid and 'quality' newspapers?

Readings 11 and 12   The Social Fund

Since the Liberal reforms of 1908 onwards there have been two principal elements to social security; on the one hand there have been National Insurance benefits to which people are eligible if they have paid sufficient contributions from their wages (or have been credited with contributions). These are paid as a right. On the other hand, there has been a means-tested scheme for those people who have not paid sufficient insurance contributions; sometimes these have been *discretionary* and sometimes people have had a *right* to such payments, for example, single payments for furniture and clothing where the appropriate need can be demonstrated. In April 1988 a new scheme was introduced which replaced Supplementary Benefits with what is known as Income Support. Family Income Supplement, for people on low wages who fall below the government's poverty line, has been replaced with Family Credit. Similarly, the system of single and urgent needs payments to which people claiming Supplementary Benefit were entitled if they could demonstrate the appropriate need has been replaced by the Social Fund.

SOCIAL FUND
The Social Fund is a scheme to help people on low income meet certain expenses which they are unable to meet from their weekly income. It replaces

★ maternity grant
★ death grant
★ single payments of supplementary benefit
★ urgent needs payment

Payments from the Social Fund may be in the form of grants or loans. They are divided into four categories:
★ payments for funeral and maternity expenses
★ community care grants
★ budgeting loans
★ crisis loans
Most payments are discretionary. Some are paid as a right.
(Adapted from National Association of Citizens Advice Bureau, Social Security Training Pack, January 1988)

Since the scheme is cash-limited, two people with identical cases may be treated differently because they apply to different DHSS offices with differing priorities, or they may apply at different times in a particular month. This is a concern for those people who are providing advice and support for claimants. It is a particular concern for social workers.

SOCIAL SECURITY AND SOCIAL WORK
The government's proposals for introducing a Social Fund as part of its 'reform' of the social security system have met with overwhelming criticism from a wide range of organisations and individuals. Opposition to the Social Fund has centred largely on two of its key elements. First, the replacement of the legal right to single payments . . . by discretionary access only, together with the abolition of the right of appeal, are widely seen as retrograde steps which would undermine human rights and principles of natural justice. Second, the wholesale replacement of many single payments by loans – in the absence of any overall improvement in weekly benefit levels – means, in effect, the imposition of a new, lower 'poverty line' on claimants. They would be expected to pay for a range of items hitherto recognised as being beyond the ability of even the best 'managers' on SB to pay for out of their weekly allowance.

But there is a third important reason for concern . . . . The proposals for the Social Fund may be seen as a worrying development in the relationship between the social security system and social work services – or 'cash and care', as they are called in the government's White Paper on the Reform of Social Security. As both CPAG [Child Poverty Action Group] and BASW [British Association of Social Workers] pointed out in their responses to the earlier Green Paper, the Social Fund proposals not only assume a degree of social work expertise on the part of Social Fund officers, but also seem to encourage the latter to approach social workers for financial help (such as section 1 payments) for their clients before considering a DHSS loan. There have also been fears that claimants may be tempted to become social work clients simply in order to gain access to such payments.

Such 'net-widening' would erode the long-standing distinction between entitlement to benefit and assessment for social work help. Moreover, social workers acting as advocates for their clients may well feel more ambivalent about this role when faced with a cash limited Social Fund in which one claimant's gain could become another's loss.

(Gill Stewart with John Stewart, *Boundary Changes: Social Work and Social Security*, Child Poverty Action Group/British Association of Social Workers, 1986.)

Questions and activities

1 What are the main characteristics of the Social Fund?
2 Write down what you consider to be the main advantages and disadvantages of (a) a system of discretionary payments, and (b) a system of payments as of right.
3 Why are social workers particularly critical of the Social Fund?

Further reading

There are numerous texts which examine particular areas of social policy such as education or housing. Also, social policies are constantly changing and it is useful to subscribe to a 'quality' newspaper in order to keep up to date. Journals and periodicals are also good sources of information and analysis such as the *Journal of Social Policy, Critical Social Policy*, and *New Statesman and Society*, as well as the more specialist periodicals such as *Community Care* and *Poverty*.

General reading

J. Dale and P. Foster, *Feminists and State Welfare*, London Routledge & Kegan Paul, 1986.
A good feminist examination of the welfare state.

V. George, and P. Wilding, *Ideology and Social Welfare*, London Routledge & Kegan Paul, rev. edn, 1985.
Despite criticisms, it is still one of the best analyses of political ideologies and social policy.

V. George, and P. Wilding, *The Impact of Social Policy*, London Routledge & Kegan Paul, 1984.
A most comprehensive study of the effectiveness of the welfare state and a good analysis of the successes and failures in social policy, although the authors tend to focus on issues of social class at the expense of other disadvantaged social groups.

M. Hill, *Understanding Social Policy*, Oxford, Basil Blackwell, 1980; 2nd edn, 1983.
A most useful introduction to the policy-making process and welfare institutions.

M. Hill, and G. Bramley, *Analysing Social Policy*, Oxford, Basil Blackwell, 1986.
A useful introduction to the study of social policy.

C. Jones, *Immigration and Social Policy in Britain*, London, Tavistock Publications, 1977.

A most useful historical study of social policy, migration and race.

R. Mishra, *Society and Social Policy*, London, Macmillan, 1977; 2nd edn, 1981.
A useful text which outlines the differing approaches to the study of social policy.

G. Pascall, *Social Policy – a Feminist Analysis*, London Tavistock Publications, 1986.
An excellent and most readable discussion of the relationship between women and social policy.

C. Phillipson, and A. Walker (eds), *Ageing and Social Policy*, London, Gower Publishing Co., 1986.
An excellent collection of articles which examine age and ageism in a number of different ways. (Its only disadvantage is that it does not address the issue of older black people.)

P. Thane, *The Foundations of the Welfare State*, London, Longman, 1982.
An excellent study of the origins of welfare, both in Britain and in other countries.

A. Walker, *Social Planning – a Strategy for Socialist Welfare*, Oxford, Basil Blackwell, 1984.
Although polemical, it provides an excellent critical discussion of the study of social policy and political values.

F. Williams, *Social Policy – a Critical Introduction*, Cambridge, Polity Press in association with Basil Blackwell, 1989.
A long overdue addition to any examination of social policy. With its focus on gender, race and class this is an essential text for anyone who wishes to study social policy in more detail.

Index